Saving Grace

My Journey & Survival through Post Natal Depression

Grace Sharrock

authorHOUSE®

AuthorHouse™ UK Ltd.
500 Avebury Boulevard
Central Milton Keynes, MK9 2BE
www.authorhouse.co.uk
Phone: 08001974150

First published by AuthorHouse 8/30/2010

ISBN: 978-1-4520-1756-3 (sc)

618. 76

This book is printed on acid-free paper.

I am writing a book about my experience of post natal depression. My kind was the severe and most rare kind. Puerperal psychosis. Following the birth of my Daughter Ellie. This book is about what happened to me, the effect it had on me, my daughter, and all those closest to me.

It is a detailed account of what can happen just from giving birth.

My daughter is now 8, and I would say 5 years of her life were very tough for me. But together we got through it.

I got in touch with a lady called Elaine Hanzak. She had the same illness through pregnancy and birth that I had, she went on to write "Eyes without Sparkle". Her account of her condition and what happened to her following the birth of her son. After speaking to her, and reading her book, she gave me the inspiration and confidence to write my story, and share my experiences with others. This condition is very rare, and until I had it, I had never heard of it. However post natal depression and puerperal psychosis is becoming more common, in new mothers.

I am writing this for mums who have experienced this illness, and Mothers who may experience this condition in the future.

Hopefully in the near future with Books, and peoples accounts of this condition being looked at and researched more closely, people will gain more insight and knowledge into this condition.

So what happened to me will not happen again, and if so dealt with better and quickly. I think if my family and friends did not know me as well as they did, the outcome of my story could have been very different.

A lot of people, including myself, before I had my daughter, do not know the signs and symptoms to look out for. Hopefully in the future more things can be done in the early stages, and people can be more aware of the effects that this condition can have on new mothers their babies, and their families. If my book helps just one person, a mother or a partner, of a person who has just had a baby it will all be worth it.

I would like to thank all the people involved in helping me to get better, and the people who have given me the strength and courage to write about what happened to me. I would like to thank firstly my Mum and Dad, who saw me go through the whole illness and were there for me even when I came home, and to this day are still there for me and my daughter now. My brothers and sisters, especially my Sister Sue, and my brother Ben. My nieces and nephews, and also my Friends, Sandy for nudging me to write and helping me make contact with other people such as Elaine Hanzak and for all the support and advice. I would especially like to thank my best friend Maria. It took a long time to get our friendship back on track, but we did and it is stronger than ever. She helped me through so much and has done always, and ever since.

I am a stronger wiser person for having gone through this experience, and I have never taken a day for granted since.

G Sharrock

ONE DAY...

A poem About Post natal Depression.

No mobiles or prams,
Or balloons and baby treats,
Just tears and sorrow and lack of sleep.

Wanting to hold her, but not knowing how?
I want to be a mummy but not right now.

My pillow is wet, as I hold her pink little bear,
I stare into space on the old rocking chair.

Her eyes of blue, so beautiful, tiny and perfect,
She was taken from me because of fear of neglect.

My heart aches when I think of her...
How could they think that I don't care?

Her smell is on her cotton sheets,
She's not there, but still I hear her crying, and long for her to go to sleep.

Mummy loves you, and is here somewhere inside,
She's trying to get out and to hold you with pride.

Mummy's little angel, mummy's little star,
I am going to get better, and I won't be very far.

I will be here when you wake, when you cry,
Not some nurse who doesn't love you, even though she does try.

Mummy will go and find her smile,
But don't worry; I won't be long ill be back in a while.

One day it will be me, who can give you a bath,
I can't wait to tickle you and make you laugh.

One day my beautiful baby,
Mummy will be here, holding you close, and I won't let go as I hold you so dear,

Grace Sharrock

1

Chapter One

FALLING IN LOVE

I grew up in Liverpool, to a working class family; I was born on the 27th September 1978. I was one of 8 children. We lived on a rough council estate and money was in short supply. But we had each other. When I say where we lived was rough, it really was. When people started throwing their dogs off the council flat block because they couldn't afford or be bothered to look after them, mum decided it was time to go.

So we moved to Cheshire. It was like a different world. The accent sounded posh to me. I remember going in to the local shop and listening to a girl ask how much the cans of coke were. She sounded so strange. Balm cakes were called baps? Amongst other things that were different, our stones throw away over the water was like another planet to me. As alien as this place was to me, I was the alien.

I had everybody taking the Mick out of my accent, and I took the Mick out of theirs, it was a long time until I settled in and before I knew it I had made lots of friends and Cheshire was my new home.

I had known him from the age of 12. He was pale and spotty and had hair like tin tin. We had grown up together, and I liked him a lot but that was all. To be honest I stayed away from boys and was more interested in my mates and school. His name was Mark, if somebody would have told me there and then he would be the man I was to fall in love with I would have laughed. We were about 15 and spending time together in and out of school. Thinking we were cool swigging white lightening cider and hanging about at the local park. I hated the taste of it; I could then and still now get drunk off the whiff of a beer mat. I just loved our little group. We weren't bad or do anything wrong we just sat and made each other laugh. We would all get together as often as we could.

It was only when other girls started to fancy him and be interested in him that I wanted him to be more than just my friend. I didn't let on but everybody knew. The time came when we could all pass for 18 and get into clubs and pubs we were only 17 really but with a bit of make up I could pass for 18. Two halves of lager and a packet of crisp later, Grace was drunk (didn't take much like I said) and as usual it would be Mark who looked after me. We ended up kissing and cuddling the whole walk to my house. He said he felt exactly the same as I did.

I remember that night so well, I got locked out (pretended to be) he walked me to his house. We kept stopping to kiss and hug each other; I had felt so many feelings for him for so long it was amazing that he felt the same and the more I was with him, the deeper I felt. I knew I was in love with him. We arrived at his mum's house at some ungodly hour. His mum, Dad and sister were asleep in bed. Like a complete gentleman he laid out his sleeping bag and got on the floor. I told him not to be silly and to cuddle up and get in with me and go to sleep; he didn't have to give up his bed. At that point his dad walked in. "Mark where the hell have you been its late"? Not realizing he had a drunk 17 year old in his bed. All I could say was "hello" and he nodded and looked at Mark as if to say I will deal with you in the morning. We giggled and curled up and went to sleep.

Being there felt right, and there was nowhere else I wanted to be.

From that moment on I was sort of adopted by his family. I was there that often that they should have charged me rent. We were together happy and in love. The time came when he was going to have to go away to university of all places Newcastle. I had had to re sit my A levels as I didn't get the grades I had expected to get. I desperately didn't want him to go, but he did and he and he didn't want to say goodbye because he thought it would be too upsetting. I walked all the way to his mum and dad's house, and watched him leave in a little blue van with all his belongings inside. I cried the whole way home. I don't know how or even why I fell in love with him, but I did and I so wanted to be with him. He had been gone a week, and he kept in touch by phone. He would ring somewhere in a queue trying to sort his grant out, and his diet consisted of super noodles, and more super noodles.

Telephone calls became less and less, and I gradually couldn't get hold of him. I left messages with his mum and dad, but no reply. I was heartbroken; I couldn't eat, sleep, or do anything. He didn't want to be with me anymore and things had changed for him, I had to get on with my life but I missed him terribly. I was retaking my A levels, and had a part time job at a wholesalers working on the till. I hated it but it gave me a little bit of money. I was dragged out by the girls from school, and I reluctantly went. Once inside the pub I saw one of his friends from school, he came over and said "hello" and told me Mark was in the loo. I had not seen him for over 5 months and my heart sank and my legs became all wobbly. I was excited and nervous all at the same time. I kept thinking thank god my hair and make up is done. Then I saw him come out of the toilet and he spotted me. He looked as nervous as I did. I wanted to run over to him and smack him one and kiss him all at the same time. I wanted to wrap my arms around him and tell him how much I missed him but how angry I was that he had cut me off. But instead I smiled and stood by the bar and ordered a drink with my heart racing.

He finally came over and asked me how I was, and we both plucked up the courage to talk to each other. We sat and talked for over two hours and he explained why he left the way he did, and if he didn't cut me off and concentrate on university, he would have ended up jacking it in and never have been able to go.

That night we made love and spent all our time together, until he had to go back. It was awful. I wanted to be with him so much. We kept in touch daily, and I decided I had to see him and have his arms around me. I asked my boss for the Saturday off and told him the urgency of my trip. He replied with "it's a weekend, and we are busy no you cannot have it off". I decided I never really did like that job and booked a ticket for the national express coach. I may just add that all I had was the name of the street he lived on, no number, and he had no idea I was coming. The only person I told was my best friend Maria who thought it was 'very romantic' and I just had to go. I knew she would understand. I rang my mum when I was about to board the bus, and lets just say she was a tad miffed. She then rang his mum who was more than pissed off. Her son was at university trying to make a better life for him and here was I ruining it for him.

I didn't care in the slightest, I loved Mark and I knew he loved me, I wanted to be close to him, and I missed him so much. I would have moved there to be near him. I didn't realize that the coach took 9 hours to get there with stops and pick ups along the way. I suffered with really bad car sickness or as it turned out bus sickness. I had my head down the vilest toilet cubicle for at least 3 of those hours. My make up had wore off and I had sick in my hair I could not have looked worse. The time eventually came when I could get off the bus and go in search of my fella.

I had the name of the street and while looking for the road I needed I thought to myself, "its one road it can't be that big'? How wrong I was, it was huge and had two sides to it with numbers going all the way up to the hundreds. I must have knocked on every door asking if he was there. I saw what looked like student accommodation and asked via a buzzer if Mark was there. She said yes and buzzed me up. I was finally here, I had lost my job, I had sick in my hair I looked a total mess, my m um was worried sick but it was all going to be worth it just to be with him if only for a few hours. I went upstairs to the distinct smell of chicken super noodles and thought I must be in the right place then. I saw couches scattered everywhere with rips in and glasses and bottles everywhere it looked a right tip. I scanned the room and there he was looking at me shocked sitting on the sofa. I

was worried that I had done the wrong thing, then his shocked expression turned into a smile and he rushed toward me with his arms open. We went into his bedroom and we didn't come out all day. We sat in bed listening to music eating m&m's. Curled up in each others arms. I told him I was sorry to comer unannounced but I missed him so much. Within a month he was home and looking for work, and he somehow managed to sort out finishing his degree whilst working. I didn't even know he was home until a huge bouquet of flowers arrived at the door with" I love you, and guess who?" on them. He rang me that night and I was thrilled. I was completely in love with him. We were together for a couple of years and decided that we wanted to buy a house of our own. We saved for what felt like ages for our deposit, and it was a hectic time. We had hardly anything when we packed up to go apart from a fridge freezer off his mum and dad as a moving in present. And an old table offs his Nan and granddad. The night we moved in we slept on a mattress as we didn't have a bed yet, and I remember watching him fall asleep thinking, "we did it" I felt like a grown up. We were only 21, we didn't have any money or belongings as such but I have never been happier. Soon after we had a big house warming party and we invited all our friends and family. I was making sure everyone was having a nice time when I looked over at Mark mopping spilled beer up with a dish cloth, and I thought we have our own house and we are together, I was so happy I felt like I could burst.

We got bits and bobs together and after a while it started to look like home, and I felt so proud that it was ours. We spent most of our time as a foursome with my best friend Maria and her then boyfriend who lived around the corner from us. We would go out, or spend time at each others houses having meals watching DVD's and having a laugh. We had our ups and downs but generally life was good and we were happy. My mum always said " you don't know somebody till you live with them". She was dead right! He was so untidy! And messy and I didn't realize it until now. But then I was always abit like Monica from friends "obsessed with cleaning" Mark would say and that name stuck and for a while it became my nickname.

Chapter Two

FINDING OUT

2000, and I found out I was pregnant in the May. I have never been one for being regular with my periods and was always early or late. It never really occurred to me that I could be. Maria and her then boyfriend Karl, decided that it was such a lovely day and we were not in work, we should go down to the beach, and we did, just the four of us. We had a lovely day messing about.

Maria We weren't in our house that long before I realized that I was pregnant. We moved in our new house on the 13th March mentioned that she was late for her period and thought she may be pregnant she wasn't. Like me she wasn't regular either. We liked the idea of flirting with possible motherhood. We were all grown up now with our own houses and partners and it was abit like we were playing house, except instead of dolls, we had wine. Just like we did in our bedrooms when we were teenagers, singing with our hairbrushes in the mirror drinking cheap wine, and singing our heads off. But this time we didn't have mums nagging us to turn the music lower we were in our own houses.

As soon as the lads were out she produced a pregnancy test. I said "what's that for" she said "how late are you" I said " I don't know about ten days". " This is madness" you know what I am like" i am always late". I sat on the couch and she pulled out a predictor test. She said "see if you are"? I laughed it off and said oh go on then" "but I wont be"! I knew I couldn't be but I played along we were both playing along. I had been with

Mark years and had always been careful. "Besides Maria, we've hardly done it lately". We ended up doing the test laughing and giggling, I was convinced that it would be negative; we could go back to our wine and wait for the boys to come home.

A minute passed and Maria's face was white. It's pink! She screamed. "Pull the other one" I said "yeah yeah" pass it here. "Grace your pregnant!!" No joke I am not messing around". "If it's pink it means I am not". No grace it means if there are two pink dots you are!! I took the test from her and looked at it. "Grace you are going to have a baby oh my god"!! "What?" "No we can't be" we have been careful" we haven't done it for ages' "it's wrong the test is wrong". Messing around was one thing but a positive test was another. "Grace, it can't be wrong, they are 99.9 percent accurate". " No" I think you mean they are 0.1 percent inaccurate". I looked at the two pink dots and burst into tears. I thought that I couldn't be pregnant. I was 21, I had no money behind me and no furniture even this was all mad, I couldn't think straight. At that point Mark's car mounted the curb, and he parked the car, as he reached for his keys I ran to the bathroom.

For some reason I thought it would be a good reason to barricade myself in the bathroom to get my thoughts together. I didn't know how I was supposed to be feeling. A baby we were so young and there was so much we wanted to do first. I didn't know how Mark would react? Would he be happy would he be sad? I just didn't know. As I was digesting all of this he walked through the door after making me unlock it. He came in and said "I made Maria tell me I was worried". "Have you done a test" he said. I nodded. He swung me round in the air and said "if I have to work 247 we will do this" this is great". He was shocked but happy. I was in total shock and did not know what to say. He told me he loved me and we made an appointment to see the doctor. I wanted to keep it between us until I had got used to the idea and made sure everything with the baby was okay and asked Mark not to say a thing. He agreed but within half an hour he wanted to tell everyone he was like a kid at Christmas. Two hours ago we were planning doing the house up and going the pub, in the next minute we were planning a family.

It was confirmed by the doctor that I was a couple of weeks pregnant. We decided to tell our parents. I rang my mum as she had moved back to Liverpool at this time. I didn't want to wait for the journey there so rang her on my mobile. I dialed the numbers in the phone and I actually started to feel less scared and became excited, we could do this I know we can. She answered the phone. My mum didn't believe me at first, she laughed and said "nice joke grace" I had to firm with her for her to believe me! My mum knew I was a planner and that I wanted to get married first, and find myself before I was knee deep in nappies. I assured her that I wasn't joking and even though the timing was wrong I was with the man I wanted to spend the rest of my life with, and even thought the timing was wrong it would be okay. She congratulated me and I promised to go over the very next day.

Within minutes the mobile was ringing and all my brothers and sisters were screaming down the phone. We then parked up to his mum's house. We got out of the car and hand in hand walked up to the door. His mum was in the kitchen chopping fruit to make a fruit salad and his dad was saving the world on his pc. Mark came in and said "we have got something to tell you". His mum swung round and said " your not pregnant are you"? We both nodded and she almost stabbed me with the knife she was chopping the fruit with she was so happy. His dad jumped up out of his seat and hugged us both and kissed me on the cheek and shook mark's hand. They couldn't believe they were going to become grandparents for the first time. The whole family, his Nan and his Granddad were so excited about becoming great grandparents too, and his Nan got straight on to making hats and booties and little cardigans. That night we lay in bed, almost shocked at how one day can change your life forever. We were so young and that did bother me, but I knew I loved him and it wasn't like we had been together five minutes. He assured me that it would be fine. He fell asleep, and I looked at my tummy, thinking that the start of a whole new life was in there and how I was going to do it all completely different. I had visions of it being glamorous and closed my eyes and visualized a Calvin Klein advert. A thin as a twig gorgeous model (that would be me) throwing a toddler in the air on a beach, and three wheeler buggies, and car seats and mobiles, and how it was all going to e just perfect. But life is not like that is it? And I was soon just going to find out.

Chapter Three

THE SICKNESS

The Sickness seemed to start almost immediately, almost as if to say "don't get too comfortable".

Reality started to kick in that things were happening in my body. We both worked full time Mark worked for a local chemical company. He measured chemicals and tested them, to be honest I didn't really know what he really did, all I know is it was a good job, an important job, and that he wore boots and a blue uniform and came home stinking to high heaven of chemicals and oil.

When we moved in to the house I hardly saw him anymore, he seemed to be on call 24 hours a day. I worked in the precinct for a credit company. I did quite well at school, and I knew I was better than what I was doing, but I had a house a baby on the way and bills to pay, I could worry about that later. It wasn't a great job really the idea was this company would give people with bad credit finance to buy big heavy goods like, washing machines and big screen TV's, basically stuff that they didn't really need at extortionate prices. I would deal with the debt, send letters out and take payments, sometimes I would get a "go fuck yourself " down the phone when they didn't pay on time. Wasn't exactly the fairytale I had dreamed of when leaving school.

It didn't help with this wave of nausea and sickness that would envelope my whole body from the minute I opened my eyes until I went to sleep. I still had to keep working and carry on but at times it was impossible. The doctor said don't worry it will pass, but it just got worse. I had to stand at the till when a customer was there, and when they had gone I would sit down behind the till. The queues could be enormous especially on a Saturday and I would be completely and utterly knackered. I had to keep a bucket under the till and when the feeling overtook me I would have to be sick in it. Sounds gross I know, but if I were to go the toilet to be sick, it happened that often I would end up staying there, getting paid to look at the bottom of the toilet bowl.

My manager was lovely, but I think he started to lose his patience when instead of giving a customer her change I threw up all over her hair and on her baby's buggy, and thank god missing the baby!

It was like the scene in poltergeist, I was sick so quick and so violently sometimes I didn't make it to the loo in time. I would spend half of the morning with my head down the loo, in the end I had to have the bucket and a pack of baby wipes with me everywhere I went. I headed off to Asda on my lunch one day from work, because I wasn't keeping anything down, once the nausea stopped I would be really hungry, but then I would eat then I would be sick and it would start all over again. I was walking in the aisles looking for 'light' foods as I was told to try and eat, and little and often when the sickness washed over me. I had left my bucket back at work and I could feel it erupting inside me. I tried to dash to the nearest loo, when an elderly lady on a motorised cart came by my way. I am ashamed to say I threw up all over the poor woman. It was like a scene from Little Britain when the two elderly ladies are sick and spray everything within reach, it was horrific. I couldn't apologise enough and tried to explain that I was pregnant but she put her motor on full speed and whizzed away from me. I went back to work and cried.

Getting up for work was torture and the cycle of sickness would start all over again. I was tired and felt constantly ill. I decided I couldn't cope with it any longer and went to the doctors. It turned out that I had actually lost weight and had key tones in my urine and basically I had no nutrients that I so needed in me. The doctor said I had to go to hospital immediately. I couldn't get hold of Mark or anyone; I ended up arriving in a taxi in floods of tears.

Once I got there I was put on a drip, and asked to lie down. I must have fallen asleep as soon as my head had hit the pillow. I had completely drained myself, and was glad of the rest.

I managed to get hold of Mark from a payphone and explained what had happened; I was dehydrated and completely shattered. They ended up giving me a scan; I was nearly 9 weeks pregnant. I saw this tiny little shadow that looked a lot like an old potato growing out the side of my womb, but that little shadow was my baby. After seeing that little life on screen, I realised I had to take better care of myself and that I wanted this baby more than ever. I was as sick as a dog but the nurse assured me that the baby, the pregnancy seemed to be coming along fine.

I was so relieved and so was Mark. The drip seemed to do me the world of good, and I was glad of the sleep and the time off work.

Once I got home, it seemed to be the start of things to come. The sickness continued and seemed to take a hold over me. I had to take vitamin and mineral supplements to make sure I was getting some of what I was missing from the food I wasn't keeping down. All my sisters had kids and had pregnancies I was an auntie at 5, I never remembered any of my sisters being this sick or it interfering with their lives in such a big way why this happening to me was? I wanted to go to ante natal classes and they were doing under water aerobics for pregnant mums down at the local pool, but I just couldn't stop throwing up. In the end it was embarrassing and the last thing I needed were people looking at me like I was a freak.

I would walk around and I would see pregnant mum's with their husbands and partners, and they looked glowing, a picture of health even. With their little bumps and smiles. I felt so jealous, they could enjoy their pregnancy and I couldn't I felt robbed of something so lovely and natural it didn't seem fair.

My nieces and nephews were lovely, I loved being with them. Especially our Emma, my elder sister Beryl's daughter. When she was little she practically lived at our house as Beryl was quite young when she had her. I remember being little and seeing my big sister's tummy grow, and up until then I hadn't really seen any babies and Emma was the first grandchild to be born. I had changed her nappy, and all the kids nappies, so I had an idea of how hard work babies can be. Times had moved on of course, and there were loads of new contraptions out for babies, 3 wheeler prams, mobiles that rock themselves, it was mind boggling. I would buy my Mother and baby magazines and look at the cute little babies and the gorgeous mum's, and reading about what milk you should use, and what you shouldn't. There was so many do's and don'ts I was dizzy with all the information. I knew in my heart I might not measure up to all these glam mums with the perfect nails and hair, but I would love my baby and give it the best start I possibly could.

I ended up going in and out of hospital a lot, on a drip, and the sickness continued, at one point I thought I was getting better, I wasn't I was just getting used to it. Throwing up and closely inspecting all nearby restaurants and peoples toilet bowls within a 10 mile radius became my life, for the next 6 months anyway.

I started to get a bump and my breasts became much bigger, I had never really had 'boobs' so it was new for me, and Mark didn't seem to mind either. They were big but very sore. I applied gels and creams and sprays all over my bump, as all the magazines and clinics advised this, so as not to get stretch marks. I need not have bothered, I must have spent hundreds on the bloody gels and creams for the good it did me. My stomach now looks like the map of china and hangs over my knickers. Lovely image as you can imagine. I remember wanting to complain as they became visible and red around the 6 to 7 month stage. I felt like I had been conned it didn't exactly do what it said on the tin. The doctor had a real gem for me when I said this he said and I quote: " if you are prone to get them, you will get them cream or no cream'. Well I went berserk! So much that does for me now then! They should have that written on the bloody creams and lotions. I would have still had stretch marks but my purse would have been abit heavier.

By 7 months the sickness eased and only raised its ugly head in they mornings. I began to make up for lost time; my appetite was back with a vengeance! And I didn't waste anytime stuffing my face. I was hungry and at last I could do what all pregnant mums do when they pregnant... EAT! Mark used to say it was ear or be eaten when he referred to me. I ate kippers, and stunk of fish, and ate pun nits and pun nits of Victoria plums. Thank god they were healthy carvings and not chocolate and burgers. My waist grew and so did I, before I knew it size 10 was a distant memory. I looked like a hamster storing food for the winter. I would look at my nice dresses and cry. By the later stages of pregnancy I can honestly say I looked like the Michelin man. The sickness was still there on and off, and if I over indulged I would throw up everywhere. It wasn't like a little bit of sick, and because I was eating now let's just say it was thick and full of whatever I had been eating, as you can imagine fish and plums in reverse, not a pretty sight.

I almost never made it to the toilet, once it came it overtook and I would be violently sick everywhere. Mark was patient at first and would hold my hair back while I threw up, and rub my back, but in the end I think I embarrassed him. I couldn't predict where or when it was going to happen, we could be in friends houses or at relatives or the shop, and it would wash over me and but I couldn't help or control it. I hated the feeling afterwards. It was like having the worst hangover of your life everyday without actually having a drink. It all got too much and I ended up sobbing down the toilet, I was sick of the smell of toilet duck and seeing my vomit before me, I would sit and cry and in the end at times I would get a pillow and fall asleep by it. Its funny I don't throw up very often, and the feeling reminds me of being pregnant.

The months passed and we were so excited about becoming a mummy and a daddy. I went mad and spent all my wages on baby clothes and mobiles and booties and basically everything you could need for a new baby. Mark used to kiss my bump and rub my belly, and before we went to sleep we would talk to the baby. We were excited and sickness or no sickness it would all be worth it to have our baby in our arms. By the 35th week of pregnancy I must have piled on at least 4 stone. I was huge! You didn't know whether to say hello to me or harpoon me. I was covered in stretch marks, and cursed every oil and cream I had ever bought. I still didn't feel too good and I was very tired and swollen. Everybody seemed to look at me like a bomb that was ticking and could go off at any second. I loaned a birthing video from my friend Pam, who had two kids of her own. I sat down with Mark. Worst mistake of my life if I wasn't completely terrified before, I definitely was now. I remember saying to Mark. " I am not doing that; it will just have to stay in there". Mark said don't be silly it will be fine. I thought so easy for you to say you don't have to go through it I do. He held my hand and said: "you can have drugs". Up until I saw the video I didn't want drugs I wanted to opt for a natural birth like they did in the magazines with birthing pools, but after seeing that poor woman screaming her head off I wasn't so sure anymore.

I remember sitting on the couch with Dave and her said that the singer 'Ella Fitzgerald' was called 'Ella Louise' I instantly liked it and so did Mark, Dave hoped for a girl as he liked the idea of him having a helping hand in his grandchild's name.

We thought of names and we both liked Ella Louise, and Jack. I thought of lots more but we couldn't agree on them. We narrowed the list down to two. We had no idea if it was a girl or a boy, either way we would be happy, as long as the baby was healthy that's all that mattered. My mum says every minute a child is born somewhere in the world everyday, and if there are no complications with mother and child it is a miracle every time. I thought that was so right, people do it every day and take it for granted. I think it's forgotten how amazing it is that a woman can carry a human being and nurture it, and protect it from the inside, until they are big enough to grasp for breath by themselves. Whether we think about it or not, it is a miracle every time.

Chapter 4

THE RASH

I was starting to get really tired and weepy, I couldn't wait for the baby to be born, and I had forgotten what it was like to sleep on my stomach or see my feet. The baby was kicking and moving about quite allot, which made me feel secure that all was okay.

Mark was constantly in work and when he was home he was on call 24 hours a day. He was either asleep when I was up, or out when I was asleep. Sometimes he would pop his head round the door of the bathroom and say hello whilst I was being sick in the loo on his way out. I felt alone, and spent most of my time on my own as I had finished work, and it was coming up to Christmas.

Because he was so exhausted from being in work or on call, he was snappy when I did see him, and I felt like I irritated him. When I did get to see him I wanted to hug him and smell him, and spend as much time with him as I possibly could. Since he had started this job we were like ships passing in the night, and he seemed so distant fro me. When we managed to talk and try to sort things out and end up having a cuddle, his phone would ring and he would have to go.

I almost wished that his phone would break or get lost, I cursed it every time it went off because it meant when it did he was away from me. The mobile would go and the overalls would go on and he would go to work, he had too. But each time he did I would just cry. I didn't realise then though that these were just the beginnings of my tears.

Christmas seemed to come and go by so quick. Every year I would see my mum and dad and brothers and sisters on Boxing Day, and Christmas day we would spend it with his mum and dad. It was something we had always done since we got together, and I must admit I loved it. It would be his mum and dad and his sister Emma and his grandparents. It was lovely his mum would cook up a feast and his dad would ask if she needed any help and hover, and basically get in the way, so she would tell him to get out of the kitchen. At this point he would pour himself a beer and save the world on his PC.

I would do my usual, helping wash the pots and pans, and load the dish washer. Half of the time I would break more than I would wash and it became like a standard joke in the house. My bump was so big; I could just about get around the table. That morning we had all sat around the Christmas tree and opened presents together.

His sister Emma had given me an ornamental pig that was carrying a baby pig. The mummy pig had dark circles around its eyes and it was feeding the baby pig from a bottle at the bottom it said: 'piggin sleepless nights'. It made me laugh. I still have it now. This would be the last Christmas as us, next Christmas me and Mark would be a family and our baby would be here. The thought of it made me feel all warm and excited, I couldn't wait.

Mark seemed to spend more and more time away from home, I missed him desperately. During the last month we were not getting on at all, it even got so bad I thought we were going to split. I asked him to quit his job. I didn't care about money we could survive on benefits for a while, I didn't care I just wanted us, and to be together like we had always been. I needed him beside me the money as much as needed it didn't seem to matter but I and he and our baby mattered more. He went mad and the suggestion, and said: "Grace was having a baby; I can't just go and quit my job". He didn't quit but he admitted that he was spending too much time away from home. He said he would talk to his boss and try and get a month off from work.

We seemed to argue allot, and it wasn't like us in all the time we had been with each other we just didn't argue, it was alien to me and I hated it. He had an opportunity to go on a weekend break with his dad and his best friend. I was massive and could go into labour at any minute. I knew he needed this time out and time away from me from work from everything, and I urged him to go. He wasn't so sure at first but I managed to convince him that I wasn't due for a few weeks and I would ring him there minute anything happened. He needed this even if he didn't realise it. He seemed a lot better when he returned, and we talked a lot about us, and that we needed to spend more time together and maybe to think about looking for another job. I remember waking up one morning and noticed that my stretch marks had become really red, itchy and sore. I tried not to scratch them but it was impossible not too, I scratched them so hard they bled. It was so painful and inflamed. I put some cream, on them and hoped it would go. I had a sleep and when I woke this mysterious rash started to appear all over different parts of my body and they became very red and inflamed also.

The next day was my hospital appointment, and I would mention the rash then. It had become even itchier overnight. My whole body was red with little lumps all over it; the only part that wasn't affected was my face. Mark got an hour off work took me in the car and came with me.

We arrived at the hospital and by this time I looked like I had been burned. I had the check up, and the nurse noticed the rash immediately, she asked me to wait and rang for the doctor. She had a worried expression that I did not like. She saw my reaction to hers and told me not to worry and that she just wanted a second opinion. Marks phone rang and he said he had to go. I couldn't believe it! I started to cry and shouted at him to turn it off and to stay with me. He said he had to go and would be back as soon as he could. When he left the tears just poured down my face. If it was anything bad I will ring him and told myself to stay calm. I dialled my mum's number from my mobile. I knew I shouldn't be ringing her in the hospital but I was too upset to care, she heard me sob down the phone I wasn't making any sense, and she said she would get the train and come and see me, it made me feel a little better.

I was waiting for the doctor to arrive, all the while thinking what the rash could be? Maybe all the creams and lotions I had rubbed on my belly had had an effect? This was my fault if only I had just not bought them; maybe I had an allergy to them? I racked my brain hoping it was nothing too serious. The doctor arrived and I told him my theory about the creams and gels. He said he didn't think so, but wanted to have a closer look. He did this and then asked another doctors opinion, at this point I became very worried, and did they even know what it was? After what seemed like an age we were onto opinion 4, and it turned out that I had a rare rash that is caused through pregnancy. And the pregnancy hormone. They said that it would go once the baby was born. But in the baby and my best interests it was best to start my pregnancy off, and have my baby induced.

I wasn't due for another week or so, and they said I should get prepared for the birth. They wanted me to have my bag ready and settle me on to a ward. I quickly rang Mark's mobile and it went straight on to answer machine. I panicked and rang his dad and he said he would try to get hold of him and in the meantime to rest. I rang mum back and she was already on her way. As I wasn't in labour I asked if I could go home and get all my things ready. I managed to get hold of Mark and he came straightaway. We got the bag and my things together, and I suddenly stopped and got very excited that the next time we would be back in the house we would be a family.

We went back to the hospital and arranged all the things that I was going to need. I was asked to put on a gown and get hooked up to a baby monitor to check the baby was okay and wasn't in any kind of distress. Everything as far as the baby was concerned seemed fine and normal. This terrible rash was causing me so much discomfort and the need to itch it was overwhelming. I looked like I belonged in a burns unit not the maternity ward. I was told that they didn't actually have cream for what it was that I had as it was rare. So the hospitals were making me some, seemed strange that they were making a cream especially for me.

I was told when in labour this would help with the itching and the redness and then when the baby eventually arrived it would disappear. It was just an unfortunate reaction to being pregnant, that what the doctor said. Pregnant and me I decided did not mix, I thought going through the sickness was bad enough. Mark was there helping me to get comfortable, and I was told that the doctor would be along to insert gel in to my vagina, this would then help induce the pregnancy causing the waters to break and therefore start labour off.

My mum and Sister Sue arrived and we were all huddled in to a little room. I remember being really hot, and very tired, and at this point the rash was unbearable.

The nurse arrived with the cream and I was told to apply it liberally all over my body, especially my tummy were it was the worst. Between my sister and my mum we managed to cover my whole body with it. It absorbed in to my skin easily. It smelled like eucalyptus and menthol, it was a thick yellow colour and it had the desired effect, except it made me shiver with cold. It tingled and as much as it helped the itching I felt my teeth chatter. It was working and all I had to concentrate on now was having our baby and everything would be fine.

I had a window in my room and when my mum, Sue or Mark wanted a break or a cigarette they would go outside and I could see them puffing away from my window. I had texted Maria and told her what was happening, as always she sent love and kisses and said she was thinking of me. Then later on I could see her standing outside my window looking at me with a big balloon, it was just like Maria. She wasn't allowed in and we were holding hands through the glass like forbidden lovers, if I wasn't in so much agony I would have laughed my head off. I told her t6o go home and said it could be hours, she said she was going nowhere and she sat outside. It was so lovely to see her face and I told her how I was feeling and all my preconceptions about the birth. The room was not what I thought it would be, it was drab and small, and as friendly as the nurses were they were in and out did what they had to and where gone again to attend to some one else. You see in the movies and in films when women have babies they still look beautiful right to the end and a few screams here and there and its all over balloons and banners and treats for the baby. They don't mention once rare rashes or throwing up for 9 months. I thought it was going to be plain sailing I realise how wrong I was and that was just the pregnancy the baby hadn't even arrived yet. My mum kept saying " the worst is over, you will be delivered and you will be fine". I kept praying that the worst was over I felt like I couldn't take much more. Maria hugged me as best she could through the open window and listened to me moan and cry, and I instantly felt better for speaking to her and seeing her face. The nurse came in and like a school girl I pulled the curtains across so she wouldn't see Maria, as she wasn't supposed to be there. I didn't want there to see her because at least I had her if I wanted by my window, it gave me so much comfort and I didn't want the nurse taking that away from me.

I went back to bed and slept. A little while later I woke up to Mark, Sue and my mum telling me that the gel would be getting inserted to help me go into labour. While pregnant I worried about having my legs akimbo for the entire world to see. I knew I had to part my legs so the gel could be inserted. With what little dignity I had left I asked everyone to leave me on my own for a while, little did I realise the finale would be less than dignified.

I opened my legs, and the doctor applied there gel. It felt uncomfortable and cold, and a bit like having a lump of jelly between my legs but I knew in order to have my baby get rid of this dreaded rash it was something id have to do. I lay on my back thinking id wait for it to kick in and then id be on my way. 6 Hours later nothing had happened. It was decided that more gel be used, and after the third attempt no more could be used as 3 times was all that could be applied. My god was this baby ever going to come out? I had had enough, and I could feel the tears stinging my face as they ran down. My mum wiped them away as quickly as they fell, and I looked up and my mum looked like she hadn't slept in days. She looked worried and I had never seen her smoke so many cigarettes. She looked like she had aged in the last 12 hours. Sue was being positive and saying all the right things and Mark just paced the floor, at one point I thought he was going to put a hole in the lino. Several hours later my water broke I was on my way to having my baby. I felt mentally drained and physically felt like I had done 3 marathons. I had never been so tired in my life. The Nurses were great and no matter how much I moaned, they were friendly and caring. Maria kept texting from outside, and it kept me going, all I had to remember was that my baby our baby would be here soon and it would all be worth it.

Chapter 5

OUR BABY

I was told that the contraction would start maybe hours apart at first and maybe not so sharp but they would get nearer together and the pain would increase however I had to be fully dilated in order to have the baby I was told that this could take a long time and it did!

It was night time now about 9ish and marks mum and dad and sister had arrived too and I remember wearing a bright blue dressing gown and having pains on the chair and marks dad offering to walk me round the hospital for a bit of exercise.

Everyone else, even mark stayed and had a break or a cup of tea or a cigarette and we walked slowly around the hospital. We talked about the baby and it was our first baby and their first grandson or granddaughter and that he couldn't't wait till he or she was born so we could all celebrate

I remember holding onto his arm thinking I cant wait either, we will all be joined and related and it made me feel very close to him and to mark and the thought of having our family excited me the more I thought of it.

His dad then said he too needed a cigarette, as I was hot I said I would come with him. When we got outside mark had popped home for a change of clothes and was parking the car. I said to his dad here's mark he said: "yes here's your mark". I smiled and hugged him and he patted my tummy and said: "our mark". The pains were coming thick and fast and I needed to get on the bed. I was starting to cry with the contractions but I wasn't fully dilated so had to bear with them with gas and air till I was.

It was starting to get late and everyone bar my mum my sister and mark waited outside. I felt like a bomb waiting to go off. The pains were unbearable and I decided I wanted an epidural and I was on a trolley like bed with a huge light above me and the doctor who performed the epidural arrived.

Just before he arrived I also had to deal with the rash again and the cream that was put on before was starting to wear off and the redness and itching was starting to come back. I had hold of my sister's hair screaming saying the contractions were hurting me and the itching was driving me insane. My mum mark and my sister all applied more this time, but I was shouting by this point rub it harder! Rub it harder! So they did.

The doctor was ready to insert the epidural into my back, I had a gown on and at this point I was nearly naked and crying and was sitting on the bed with my arms and legs wrapped around mark while he did it, and so to hold me to keep still. It worked and within minutes the pain had gone and it could get topped up by the squeeze of a little button every 15 minutes. I could feel the trickle of the anesthetic down my back it felt cold but not having that pain was great and I think I told the doctor that I loved him at that point.

I suddenly felt very tired and wanted to sleep but couldn't't as I had a baby to push out.

It was now in the middle of the night and the baby had not yet been born. I remember lying down with mark and my sister on one side of me and my mum on the other with the midwife in front asking me to push. I did but to no avail the baby would just not come out, even though I now had no pain my tummy was very hard and very heavy and I just wanted it to be over. It was nearly morning and the night duty staff was swapping over to the day duty midwives. I was so tired at this point and wanted the baby to come more than ever.

I was taken to theatre were I was told that they would try and get the baby out with the help of forceps and if that didn't't work I would have to have a caesarean. Mark had his hat and gown on like the doctors and nurses and at one point one of the nurses asked him to sign something calling him doctor. He laughed and said: "no I am the dad sorry". We laughed and waited for our new arrival. The forceps were used they looked like huge scissors but without sharp edges, I was horrified but I didn't't care I just wanted it to be over. They tugged and heaved a few times and then the moment was upon us.

The head was out we were told, and then the baby a second or two later. They pulled the baby out I could see the baby's face and eyes were open but no crying they took the baby away and tapped the baby's back and checked everything that should be there was.

It was then that I heard a little squeak and this little bundle was passed to Mark and then me. "We have got a little girl" he said and "she's perfect". Her eyes were as blue as id ever seen, she had the most perfectly formed nose and mouth and jet black tufts of hair on her head. I burst into tears and so did Mark and so did the baby! She was here. It was like I had always had her, I didn't think I had experienced any feeling of love like I did right now, I was overwhelmed.

I remember her getting taken from me again while I got stitched up, I had to have an episiotomy (she had cut me from inside whilst being delivered) and I had to have a lot of stitches inside and out. While they stitched me up I felt like a piece of coursework! As the medical students were now there too. As far as I was concerned there were too many people I didn't know looking at my rude bits. As I was getting stitched up, the person who was doing the stitching was asking the others to come and have a look at his sewing skills! I suppose everyone has to learn I just wanted my baby a cup of tea, a shower and a long sleep. I was moved to the recovery room with the baby were there were lots of nurses and doctors about as the birth had been long and traumatic, and with the rash being so bad I guess they wanted to keep an eye on us.

Our little girl was perfect, and asleep in the transparent cot next to me. I did not feel good I didn't know what didn't feel right id never had a baby before so it was all new, but I remember not feeling good. I couldn't get my breath and my chest hurt, my sister mum and Mark could sense that something was wrong; I pushed the button by my bed to alert the nurse. Mark was already out the room trying to look for a nurse.

The doctor seemed to come almost immediately, there was something wrong with my heart and all I knew was that I couldn't' breathe properly and I was very hot. I was scared, the doctor gave me an injection in my chest and within minutes I felt a lot better it had something to do with my blood pressure being high and shock from giving birth. After the injection I slept and slept. When I woke marks mum dad and sister were there and all standing over the baby they hadn't realized I had woken up.

Mark turned to me and said:" hello stranger you have been asleep for hours" I got kissed by everyone and Mark proudly showed off his daughter to the proud grandparents and aunty. It was all to be a first for his family as I was one of 8 and my mum and dad already had 15 grandchildren! So it was more special as it was there first grandchild, and his sister at being a first time aunty, and of course our first time at being a mummy and a daddy.

I remembered buying booties one said 50% mummy and one said 50% daddy I couldn't't wait to put them on her. The rash was subsiding but still there and my tummy was still very swollen. I had decided early on that I was going to breast feed I was also told it would help regain my figure so it was good for my girl and good for me. When pregnant we thought of lots of names but couldn't sseem to agree on any. Apart from the two we had agreed on. Dave remembered the name Ella Louise. I still loved it accept we changed it slightly she didn't't look like an Ella but Ellie seemed to suit her perfectly, so we named her Ellie Louise.

She took to breast feeding really well and as id finished feeding her with one breast she seemed to be ready for the other! My boobs were huge I looked like Jordan! And I think I had more chins than a Chinese phonebook I couldn't't wait to lose the weight Id gained I didn't't like the way I looked but at that time I really didn't't care Ellie was perfect and I would look at her when she slept she looked so beautiful and I couldn't't believe something so perfect came out of my body. At least she was okay even if my body was falling apart.

I got moved onto the ward and Mark had gone home to get some sleep and to have a shower. He came back with a bag and a card and a huge bouquet of flowers and on the card it said: "Thank you for my lovely daughter I love you". Inside the bag was a pig ornament and on it said "it's a girl"! I hugged him, and kissed him and we held hands as we looked at our daughter asleep in the cot next to us. At that moment id never felt so close to him and so happy it was all I could ever want.

I couldn't't wait to get a shower and make myself look a bit more presentable. Ellie had to go in a room with all the other babies and it had to be locked when I wanted to leave her or get a shower but there was a huge window so the nurses and midwives could see the babies, and the nurses would go in every now and then to check on them all until all the mums came back from having smokes or showers.

I felt my first time at being a mum and not wanting to leave my baby. I took a picture of me and mark out of my bag and directed it at Ellies face and taped it onto the cot. It sounds silly now as she couldn't't even see properly yet! But it made me feel better about leaving her.

I walked to the shower with my bath bag and towel I couldn't' wait to clean myself up. As the water hit my body I noticed I was till bleeding and all mums after birth tend to do that for a few weeks till everything settles back down. Except I looked down and noticed that I felt very heavy, and could feel a large amount of discharge coming out of me and then I saw this huge red lump of what looked like jelly come out of me and plopped on the floor of the shower, it looked so disgusting and red with blood.

I was shocked and immediately rang the nurse's bell on the cord inside the cubicle of the shower. I sat there thinking what now? I can't take n anymore problems this had to be the worst pregnancy and labor in history. Instantly a nurse came and saw what was on the floor and asked me if I was in any pain, I said I was okay but didn't't feel too good but id just had a baby wasn't I supposed to feel that way? I finished drying myself and changed and the nurses put the jelly onto a sick bowl as they said they would need to inspect it.

I was told it was a clot of blood, and bits from the afterbirth they thought. They took me down to have an ultra sound, it had turned out that they had left some of the afterbirth inside me and I would need to have a d and c. Basically it meant that they would have to put me to sleep and take out what was left through my vagina. I couldn't believe it, more complications what else I had had enough. The stitches I had done from the birth would all have to be undone as they would have to do the D and C and get rid of the last of it from that entrance. I would have to go through the healing process all over again.

I went down and had the procedure and was groggy and tired but it was done and I could start to heal, feel better and then go home with my new family I couldn't't wait. I was on the ward having lots of visitors, friends and family, his side my side. Flowers, balloons, cards, and banners everyone made a fuss of the baby, of me, and of Mark. It was lovely showing her off and the one thing that went well was breastfeeding.

She latched on and it couldn't' be better, but I was Still very tired. I remember being in bed and it was late, in the middle of the night infect, and I was throwing up beside my bed. Ellie was asleep and I tried to keep the noise down to keep it that way. I didn't't feel good at all, and I noticed that I had a rather large hard lump sticking out of my belly. I decided to push the button for the nurse. She came almost immediately and I told her how I felt and she saw my tummy. She said it was best if the doctor on call would come see it.

It turned out that my bowels were emptying themselves on the inside, I had not been to the toilet for a number two for days, and it was probably one of the reasons I was sick. They gave me some lactulose syrup and I had full blown diarrhoea not long after taking it. I sobbed could this get any worse? I had to wear a nappy so I could have a break from going to the toilet as I seemed to be going all the time. I was told it would pass and the medicine would clear me out and I just had to wade it out and I would be fine.

I still had the rash and marks all over me from where I was itching and every orifice was hurting or red or both. All in all I didn't feel in great shape, but I soon would be fine and home I hoped.

Id been in hospital by this point now a few days. Most new mothers these days are sent home if all is ok the day after. The sister of the ward was a big woman quite bossy and was telling me to move around a bit more and telling me repeatedly that I wouldn't't have the nurses on hand when I went home. It was such a difference from the staff that looked after me when I was in Labor they were lovely and full of love and support. They would make jokes and prop my pillows up, making sure I had everything that I needed. Even the cleaners were lovely and friendly, and regaled me of stories when they had had their children.

I felt like this nurse didn't care, she needed the bed, I was a number not a person, I couldn't wait to get out. If I had been in the right frame of mind I think I would have told her to go and whistle, and give her a piece of my mind, but I didn't. I was so unbelievably drained and shattered physically and mentally I did what I was told. But looking back on it makes me so angry that she could get away with that because I was so fragile and too weak to say anything, when I was obviously so unwell and had been through what should have been the most amazing experience of my life.

As much as it was amazing seeing my daughter born and something I will never forget, the staff that look after you and your baby are such a vital part of what you remember, and at times I felt like it was like a conveyer belt system of care, which saddens me as it ruins precious memories and moments that stay with you. I would love to go back and tell that lady that, and wonder if she would care?

Everything physically seemed to be okay and I was told that the following day I could go home. I looked at the other mums and their babies, and everything seemed great for them, they had big smiling faces, and seemed to have their babies and go home. I had been in longer than any of the other mums who arrived even after me. It didn't seem fair. The nurses asked me about my sores and my aches and my pains, but nobody really ever asked me how I was? Or how I felt. With the nurses it felt like I was getting a "pull yourself together" response to my tears or my 'happiness'. The birth had been very traumatic and I wanted to talk about what went wrong, how come I had all these things happen? But I was told by Mum and Sue and Mark, even the staff to not worry and that the worst was over to look to the future and my baby and my family. I wanted to do that of course but in my own head I also wanted to make sense of what had happened.

I didn't fully understand what had happened and how I was feeling afterwards, I just knew I didn't feel right, I didn't feel like Grace, I felt strange and I couldn't put my finger on it. I put it down to a traumatic pregnancy, birth, and being so ill after she was born, I just knew I had to keep going and all would be fine, that's all I kept hearing "you will be fine".

My tears would come and I didn't know where they would come from? My mum said it was natural to be like this even when things go right after having a baby, and because things had been so not right from the word go, she reckoned that added to all the pressure. I got hugs and kisses from everyone, but didn't get time to speak about anything. I had a baby now and had to get better for me and for her. The priority was the physical side and as soon as that looked like it was on an even keel, I felt like the hospital practically kicked me out of my bed.

I went home and everything seemed to be okay apart from not feeling myself completely, being sore from the stitches and lack of sleep but ok, in good spirits considering, and looking forward to my new family. All in all apart from my gorgeous daughter the whole experience was draining, horrific almost and I physically went through it. Looking back when I was pregnant and remembering all the baby books that I had read, it all now seemed like a lie. Everything that could go wrong went wrong, and I felt crushed.

I thought I could concentrate on healing and getting better and being with my new family. I remember whilst being in hospital that I was either in floods of tears or really high? Never in between, but I thought that was normal after giving birth and everybody gets baby blues don't they?

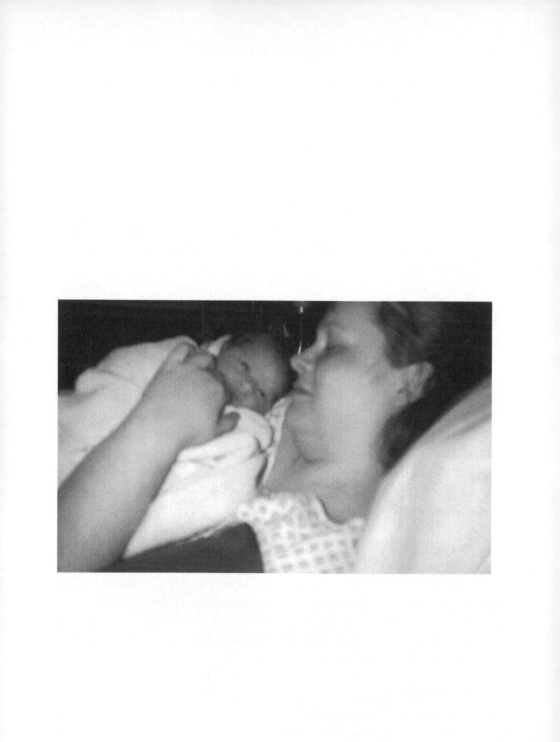

Chapter 6

WHAT'S HAPPENING TO ME?

Mark came in his car and parked at the side of the entrance and opened the door for me and his new daughter, seeing the car seat all set up in the car made me smile. We were in the back while she slept.

I wouldn't let it drop about the baby needing her own washing basket that it was important and she should have her own baby comfort I wouldn't't let up you would think I would want to get home and go to sleep but I made him stop at the shopping centre to buy one and id wait in the car with the baby. I was almost obsessed about it. He went and got the basket and we drove home. When I got in I introduced our girl to our house it was clean and tidy and mark had bought new big fluffy pillows for the couch and chairs. The house looked different and felt different. Everything felt kind of strange and new.

I went to bed and put Ellie in her carry cot next to me asleep, I must have stayed asleep for hours, I couldn't seem to stay awake, I was glad of my bed and the comfort of the duvet around me. The midwife came and checked on us both and friends and family appeared at the door too it was nice to be home. That night when everybody disappeared and went home it was just me Mark and Ellie and that suited me just fine. She had not had her first bath and we done it together, we were both so nervous and excited.

Ellie screamed the place down; as we lowered her body into the water it felt lovely that it was just us. The three of us went to bed early and I woke with Ellie to breastfeed every couple of hours. Mark sat up in bed next to me fascinated and watched as Ellie latched on. She sucked so hard we could see the milk flowing at the side of her mouth; it was so natural and so lovely, at

That point I didn't't think I could be happier than I was right there And then.

The next day my mum and my two older sisters were coming from Liverpool to visit with my two nieces. My mum kept asking me if I was okay and she commented on how untidy the house was. It was spick and span and lovely when I and Ellie came home, and normally I tidied as I went along and put things away as I used them. I was fanatical about putting things away and being tidy and clean it drove everybody bonkers, and it was not like me for it to be so untidy but id just had a baby, it didn't seem important now. But looking around the room, I could see what she meant, everything was everywhere.

My mum said I didn't't look right I said I was tired but okay. They all left with hugs and kisses for me and the baby and for mark and then they left. I went for a sleep on the couch and mark awoke me for something to eat he had made me tomato soup and left it on a table for me with some bread I was trying to use the phone but the battery had gone and Mark said he could hear me talking to myself when he came in, and asked who I was talking to? I had this rage inside me I was suddenly so very angry and felt I had a right to be angry at Mark. I threw the soup at him and the bowl smashed against the wall. I started to scream at the top of my lungs and began to hit

Him.

Mark looked so shocked he stood there for a moment before saying "what the hell are you doing"!?" what's wrong"?" grace what's wrong"? I replied with: "Who is she?" who have you been sleeping with"? Its Maria isn't it? Maria was my best friend and lived around the corner from me with her then fiancé; we had all known each other for years. Apart from Mark she was probably the closest person to me. Mark shouted "of course i am not!! "What are you on about"? My voice grew louder with anger that even shocked me. It was like I was possessed only I didn't realize it. "You are your sleeping with someone"! I bellowed at him. I began to smash all the plates in the house Ellie was crying in her pram. We didn't't realize it but it was the beginning of something nobody could ever imagine.

I suddenly didn't't feel myself at all I smashed everything I could get my hands on. I was so angry but didn't know why? And my mood was completely irrational; I was either very high or very low. I could hear the plates shattering against the wall and the cups. Ellie was screaming in her pram, I just wasn't interested, it was like I had this fire inside of me and if I didn't't react my head would explode.

Mark tried desperately to calm me down "what are you talking about grace"? "Where has all this come from"? "Sit down". "No I won't fucking sit down"! I yelled at him. It was very rare that I swore anyway, so it was as much as a surprise to me as it was to him. Then I started to run at the man I loved more dearly than anything or anyone. I rained blows on him thick and fast, and all he could do was put up his hands in protest. I started to kick scratch bite anything just to let him know how much he had hurt me and how I was feeling inside.

I felt so mixed up in my head and I wanted to run away from myself, I didn't't know what to do. He suddenly grabbed me and put his feet under my legs to get me to trip and fall to the floor to stop me from hurting him and my self. As I fell and hit the floor my ankle twisted and the pain was awful it was just badly sprained but I cried like a baby or a little girl that had just grazed her knee in the park. Then Mark started to laugh, when I started to shout: "I have broken my fucking leg!! "You have broke my leg you bastard". Looking back in hindsight it was probably a mixture of nerves and confusion that made him laugh, then I started to laugh too, more than Mark, and the look on his face told me that he was not laughing anymore and this was no joke something was seriously wrong with me.

This was more than just the baby blues. I kept repeating and repeating over and over again that he had been sleeping with my best mate and that I was going to kill him and kill her. He decided to ring Maria and get her to speak to me on the phone she was the closest person to me that you could get and if anybody could talk sense to me she could, But as he passed me the phone all my anger was directed at mark and then the next thing Maria was my best friend again, and I was shouting again saying; "I knew it Maria I fucking knew it" "was that whore! She's already taken one boyfriend now she wants this one as well"!!! "Are you going to help me kill her or what"? Maria asked who the hell I was talking about and I referred to a name that I had not used in a long time before I had met mark and fell in love with him I had a first not serious boyfriend called Paul we dated for about 3 months I was upset when it ended but it was puppy love and we kissed each other and held hands that was it! I hadn't thought about him for years? It was completely out of the blue.

But when I was seeing this Paul there was a girl in school called Helen who actually got off with him behind my back so to speak and we parted. Silly school kid stuff. The name was never really mentioned again now years later out the blue, her name came from nowhere and Maria didn't't even now who she was as she had left school by then so she was obviously very confused. But mark was right on the ball and knew exactly what I was talking about. "It's all rubbish grace you're not making sense at all"? "Give me the phone and let me talk to her". We wrestled with the phone but I would not budge. Then the phone started to beep and flash like it does when it just needs charging. It flashed went off then came back on again. I started to scream even more hysterically by this time, and said that it was the devil trying to get to me and he was coming for me and the red flash and beep was the signal for

It.

I saw the entire colour drain from marks face as I said it. Mark was very worried by this point, and became even more worried when I said things like; "but its okay god won't let that happen he loves us mark". It was as if grace was possessed like something or someone had taken over me and I was no longer me I was like a zombie. The tears started to roll down his face and before the charge went on the phone he managed to get hold of my sister and tell her what was happening and that she needed to get here fast. As this was happening I left Ellie in her pram and was heading for the door, as I got to it and opened it all the neighbours were in the street and obviously heard what was going on and came to see what was happening.

Two married men of whom I was friends with there wives, had come over and I started to laugh and flirt with them like nothing had happened? I didn't't know how to flirt! And what a situation to do it in? It was all very strange, they must have sensed something was very wrong, as the more I talked the more they backed off in to the street to get to the opposite side of the road where they lived.

One of the women came over and started to clean the pieces of plate and cups that I had smashed earlier on. Ellie was screaming at the top of her lungs in the background and I didn't't seem to care or be interested at all. It was as if I was there, but somewhere else at the same time. I headed for the door, neighbour picking up debris off the floor and Mark in hot pursuit. I heard him say that he has called for a doctor and to please wait here with the baby to the neighbour. I decided that I didn't't like the neighbour being there and told her so, shouting as hard as I could with as many swear words that came to mind. She quickly left. Mark kept telling me the doctor, my mum, and Sue was on the way. I raced out of the door with a jumper on, no shoes and my pajama bottoms, bleeding still after the birth, without a maternity towel on. I must have looked a sight. Mark left Ellie with the neighbour while he chased after me, but I was too strong for him to hold down and too quick.

He came running after me and followed me in hot pursuit. I was pacing down the street and telling him to "fuckoff" and what a "horrible lying cheating twat" he was, and how it was "all over" and I started to sob, loud heavy sobs, with tears rolling down my face. I started to shout; "I am going to Maria and Karl's house" "and I am going to rip that bitches head off" and tell her exactly what I thought of her"! Only less than an hour ago, I was having a chat with her telling her how I was going to smack Helen who had been 'cheating' with my fella. I was so very confused and so angry, but didn't't seemed to have any of the facts and or whom I was actually angry with?

Mark gave up chasing after me and decided he had better get back to Ellie, and without me knowing he rang Karl Maria's fiancé and told him that I was on my way round and to not let me in at all under any circumstances,

And to try and keep me there until my family arrived. I was hysterical and stomped my way round, uncontrollably crying along the way. I got to the door and knocked on it as loudly as I could shouting Karl's name and to let me in right now or else. The swear words were loud and thick and fast, and it must have been on show as people from the flats started to shout things, and of course I replied with a "fuckoff". An elderly couple lived next door to my best friend and the lady came out, to tell me to be on my way unaware of my mental state, and must of thought I was some young woman that had been scorned and that if I didn't quieten down or leave she would ring the police. I was right up to this elderly woman's face and swearing all obscenities at this frail old woman then suddenly her husband came out telling me to clear off and slapping me at the same time he told me that he was going to get the police. I replied by swearing again and made my way round the back of the house.

I could see into the kitchen then started to shout Karl's name to come out and speak to me. He spoke and told me that Maria was not there, and to calm down and go home to Mark. I decided since I was getting nowhere id smash the potted plants in the garden one by one in the little ceramic terracotta pots they were placed in. there must have been 5 or 6 pots quite big and I remember it being a struggle to pick them up and lift them off the floor but somehow I did and sent the flowers to the wall smashing the pot they were placed in. Karl was standing at the kitchen window wondering what the hell I was doing. I asked again and again for him to open the door but he wisely refused. At this point I was so frustrated at not seeing Maria or getting any answers I picked a pot up and started to smash the windows in the shed. At which point Karl came out and said; "Grace stop it" "what the hell are you doing"? "What's going on?" "Let me in I" said "where is that bitch"? Karl replied; "she's done nothing wrong"? "Listen to me, "you're confused and she's not here". "Let me come in" and wait then"? I said, at which point he put his foot by the door and said "no". I then calmed right down and put my arms around Karl. "I know you have always fancied me"? I said, "Do you think about me when you're with Maria"? He looked so shocked he didn't' answer. 'He removed my arms from my waist. I said; "let's be together" and Maria can have Mark" whatdja say"? He looked at me like I was insane. What the hell was I doing??? I was there to sort out a supposed 'affair' with my best mate, and the man I had just had my new baby girl too, whom I loved more than life and wanted to marry? I had never ever thought of Karl like that ever, he was my friend I was in love with Mark and he was also my best friend's fiancé? What the hell was going on when did the switch happen? He told me to leave, at which point I wanted Mark, and began to sob

On the pavement.

My feet felt cold as it was March, and I could feel small stones by the gutter touching my toes. I sat there for a moment and started to cry and shake. I looked up at people walking past looking at me and wondering what the hell I was doing there in the street with blood on the back of my pants and no shoes on. I got up and felt dizzy, and everything stared to spin. Then in the corner of my eye I saw my best friend coming towards me in her car to get to her road. I suddenly stopped crying, and anger and hatred filled me out of nowhere? I raced over to her car and she wound the window down as I approached she smiled, and as I reached her car door she suddenly stopped smiling and looked at me in horror. With glazed eyes as she recalls I looked at her and said to her; "never speak to me again" and that id kill her.

I walked past the car and crossed the road, I was so alone and scared I had no idea where I was going what I was doing, what I was feeling, and the only person I wanted was Mark, but I was so convinced he had betrayed me I couldn't' bear to look at him, I was so confused. The tears started to roll down my cheeks and the sobbing began. I was outside the local chemist that was near where I grew up, when I lived with my mum and dad. The chemist was a nice man and his wife was a solicitor and she ran an office upstairs and he run the chemist downstairs id been going there for years to buy throat lozenges or get my antibiotics when I was ill with my mum when I was off school and he knew me by first name terms.

I was standing outside sobbing and tugging at my clothes, he must have heard as he came out of the shop and shouted me. He came rushing over and picked me up and cradled me into the chemist asking me what was the matter and that everything was going to be alright. I was very muddled up and began having a conversation with myself and him at the same time. He looked at me and then at his assistant and asked her to cover the counter. I was sat on a chair in the back and his wife came running down the stairs "what's going on"? He spoke to her in whispers, as if me was't there. "What's your mum's phone number grace can you remember"? Of course I could remember I was't a fool so I gave it to him telling him this. He then rang and my mum answered. Telling the chemist thank you so much for keeping me there and that everyone was looking for me, and the police had been called and my brother and sister was looking for me.

He decided to take me upstairs and get me to lie down his wife in tow, I told him that I wanted him to stay with me, his wife didn't' seem so keen on that idea and decided I should be left alone to lie down until my family came, and they both went downstairs. I was curled up in a ball with my legs hunched up on the couch my arms wrapped around myself, rocking backwards and forwards. Then the door opened and my big brother walked in with a very concerned look on his face. Ben picked me up and took me to his car. I then had a conversation with him at how much I loved him and that everything was going to be alright. We entered my street were the police were, my brother told me not to get out the car and to stay with him and let him smooth things over. I refused at which point a policeman tapped on the window and my brother wound it down. "What seems to be the problem here"? "We have had a call off a number of people with disturbances in this area about a girl matching your description"? My brother pointed out that id just had a baby and that it was a domestic and everything was fine. He didn't' seem convinced but my brother talked some more and then the police were on there way. Little did I realize that the police were the last of my problems?

They rang the doctor immediately.

The doctor came he was a middle aged man I would say in his fifties, with grey hair balding at the top, dressed in a suit carrying his doctor's bag. As soon as he came in I told him I didn't't want to see him and to "fuckoff" at the top of my lungs, I began to grab hold of my hair and pull it, and slumped down into the corner of the room against the wall. Tears streaming down my face, he quickly left and decided I needed urgent medical help.

Chapter 7

Sectioned

I didn't realise that the disturbance in the street was me. The doctor had gone and all the neighbours were in the street watching as if it was a really good soap opera except it was real and happening to me. I remember things in vivid detail, and other memories are like a dream, and when I think back I don't think of it as being me who did or said those things. I was literally climbing the walls.

I was pulling my hair from the root, and hanging onto the door frame. The next thing I remember was my sister Sue turning up, she was crying, and I asked her if she was okay. If it wasn't so tragic it would have been funny in a way, but it wasn't. I was told I had to be sectioned under the mental health act and needed hospital treatment urgently. My family had signed a form to say that they were the ones who would be taking me. One second I was crying hysterically, the next I was very friendly or unhappy but in a very inappropriate way. I was told I had tried to touch my own brother up and even tried to kiss him. How sick is that when I think back, but I didn't know what or why I was doing anything anymore nothing made any sense. I told him that I was in love with him. It was all so mad so strange and unreal and it affected everybody around me. Nobody knew what to do or what to say to me or to themselves. Nothing like this had ever happened in my family before and nobody knew anything about what I was suffering with. I just looked like I was totally mad.

It was like someone had shook my brain, and all the things that made me Grace, were not in the right boxes inside my

Head, it was like I was there but not really there.

Mark looked so bad, and looking back I feel for him so much, he had no idea what was happening, and what should have been the happiest time of our life became the worst. We were very young 22, and looking back I wish someone would have hugged him for me, because I wasn't capable of doing it myself. Ben reassured Mark that I would be fine and that he go and get some sleep and to have a break with his mum and dad at their house. He didn't need persuading and he left and went. Ben got Ellie and we went to Ben's house. They had 24 hours to get me to hospital and they didn't know what else to do. I think they thought the longer they held on to me the better I would be. They drove to my Brothers house.

There seemed to be so many people at his house, and all the family started to turn up. Mark wanted to come just to make sure I was okay and then he was going to drive back home. I began shouting and talking very loudly, and Mark kept telling me to be quiet. But I couldn't I had to do it, and I had no control over what was cooing out of my mouth. If I wasn't talking loudly I was laughing hysterically, or crying, or being very aggressive and angry. Each emotion seemed to happen within a split second of one another.

My sisters realised that none of us had eaten all day, and there was noting to eat in brothers house so they decided to get something from the chippy. They came back with the chips and fish, and greasy sausages etc, I said to my sister Tracey that I just wanted chips nothing more. She handed me a plate full with tomato sauce on them just like I liked them. I complained that they had blood on them, and that it was god's blood.

Everybody completely freaked out, and could not understand what was happening to me. At this point my Mum started to cry. As she did so I told her not to worry because I was Mary, Mark was Joseph, and Ellie was Jesus, and that we would look after her, at hearing this she began to cry even louder.

I sat eating chips on the floor with everyone looking at me. My sister offered me a fork as she noticed I was eating with my hands. I angrily refused and said; "this is how people eat in the bible". I looked around and wondered what all the fuss was about and why were they all crying? I realise of course now that they were desperately worried and wondered what the hell was wrong with me and if id ever get better. Everybody went home to have a break Sue and Ben and his then fiancé Michaela stayed and watched me. Ben's daughter Taylor was not even 1, and Michaela was trying to care for her as well as my new born baby. They thought it was best I not be parted from Ellie, as they didn't know how long I could care for her or be with her once I got to the hospital.

Michaela was trying to get her to feed from a bottle, and to sleep but she was having none of it, she wanted her mummy, but mummy was nowhere to be seen, she was a broken shell on the floor making no sense at all. I couldn't pick her up or cradle her I couldn't even sit up and look after myself let alone her. Michaela was tired looking after the two babies and it was getting dark, I was freaking out in her house, and each time she got the babies to sleep, I would scream or shout and wake them up and she would have to try and soothe them all over again. Every time she came down the stairs I would put my hands round her neck and hit her, and scream at her and tell her she was evil. She couldn't even go downstairs in her own house.

Seeing her made me worse and what I said must have upset her so Ben told her to stay up there with the babies for their protection and her own. Ben made endless cups of tea that didn't get drunk; I think it was more of a case of something to do rather than anyone wanting one. I began getting tired and slept on the floor for a while. Ben and Sue were in the living room with me and were on the two couches looking at me. Trying to talk to me to try and find out exactly how sick I was. I sat on the floor and began talking to the fire place, I believed I could hear voices, hear Marks voice, and ended up having a conversation with it. After a while I kissed it goodnight and lay down beside it and went sleep. I

It was in the middle of the night that I woke up, and Ben and Sue were asleep. I leaned over and kissed my brother, and covered him with a blanket that was meant for me that hadn't been used and kissed him on his head, he didn't wake. I then went over to Sue, I looked at her face and all I could see was evil, pure evil, and that I had to stop her from being evil. I placed my hands around her neck, I could feel her pulse through my fingers, and placed my face very close to hers, and began to grip her neck tightly. She woke up almost immediately and her eyes were bulging out of her head and image I will never forget. I could see the look of fear in her eyes as she struggled to push me off. I tightened my grip even harder and a gurgling sound escaped from her mouth. I got on top of her and the sister that I loved who had always helped me, I tried to strangle with my bare hands.

She began kicking and managed to knock something over; Ben woke up and dragged me off her. He had to hit me several times to get me off her. She was breathing hard and looked shocked. He checked she was okay and told her to go upstairs, nobody slept after that.

They knew straight away now that I had to be admitted, I was desperately sick from having Ellie, they didn't know why or how it happened, they just knew it was bigger than them and something that they could not deal with. I think they thought that admitting I was sick and realising that I had to sectioned was in a way having to admit how sick I was, and that they were abandoning me. But they hadn't they had done everything that they possibly could; it was up to the experts to help me now. If they didn't know me as well as they did the outcome of what happened could have been so much worse. The next day we went to the main hospital just outside Cheshire with my mum and Mark. Ellie was left with my sister Tracey near by. In the car on the journey I was very erratic, opening and closing windows, fidgeting, moving when I didn't need to, looking out of the window like a child with ADHD, I was all over the place. When I got to the hospital my behaviour became even stranger and worsened. I asked everyone to go and became uncontrollable, I swore at everyone and I looked at my mum and said; "why don't you just die like me Nan". I hit my sister Sue in the face. The nursing staff arrived and gave me an injection once they strapped me to the bed. They held me by force and waited for the drugs to kick in. The best thing I remember was waking up crying. I was still strapped to the bed and the door was closed and locked. The room was small with no windows the light was on and there was a bed on a trolley that I was lying in and a thick metal door with a window in the middle with thick glass.   It looked like a padded cell without the padding. The kind you would see on telly except this was real.

Mark had gone, and so had my family I was completely alone and terrified. A nurse entered the room and asked me if I was okay and if I would like a drink. I responded by telling her to go " fuck yourself". And to leave me alone. I began shouting for Mark over and over again. I remember thinking "what's happening to me"? "Where's the baby I had"? And "why am I chained to the bed"? The hostility and aggression and utter emotion was gone from me and all that was left was this broken girl full of drugs, I was calm but Grace was nowhere to be seen, I was a zombie.

Chapter 8

THE NUT HOUSE

I remember being in the bed and I somehow must have fallen asleep. I woke up knowing that it was daytime and not night, was weird really as there were no windows in the room that they put me in but I just knew. Nurses and health care assistants would frequently come in and out. Some were young and looked like they were training and looked terrified, others looked as hard as nails and looked like they had seen and heard it all, almost expected it even. Once they gave me my medication I could go and walk around and talk to people if I wanted too. Meds consisted of two small cups one with water, and one with an empty beaker, very small with a pill or two inside. I remember looking at it and thinking; "well you can fuckoff coz that's not going in my mouth", and I would throw the water over the nurse or put the pill in my mouth and spit it out at her, like it was chewy getting spat out of my mouth. That would happen repeatedly, and they grew quite tired of it very quickly.

I remember eventually taking my meds, and then walking around the ward. I was like a child on their first day of school. It was all new and strange, and a fake clean smell of cheap lemon disinfectant hung in the air. I walked around my new environment like a rabbit caught in head lights. Whilst all of this was happening I didn't't know who anyone was, I wanted Mark and Ellie and when I thought about them it made me cry, and I felt scared, so I decided I was't going to think about them for now.

There was a long corridor which had rooms coming off them and the rooms didn't't look like wards of a normal hospital; they looked like bedrooms with one bed inside. There was a smoking room, and a huge grassy area outside. I knew that the people that worked there had smart clothes on and wore badges with their names with their pictures on of them, on a chain around their neck. That meant that all these other people were crazy or mad like me? Had they had a baby and went a bit mad too I thought? Does this happen to everyone who has a baby? I saw a lady standing by the glass door standing on the opposite side of it, puffing away on a cigarette, she didn't't look that old but time had not been kind to her she had large dark circles around her eyes, her hair was limp and greasy and she looked like she had been crying. I looked at her and tried to smile; she looked at me and looked away. In the grassy area was a young lad, or definitely a young man not much older or possibly even younger than me. For some reason this made me feel better.

He was kicking a ball outside on the grassy bit against the wall, he didn't't look very happy. The door opened and there was an older man with glasses on and very greying hair, in a dressing gown looking at me asking me what I was in for? I said I didn't' know really, and asked where there was water or somewhere to get a drink? He said there was a tea and coffee machine but that it tasted like shit. I reluctantly went and got one and he was right it really did taste bad, but it was Luke warm and wet, and would do for now, till I figured out what I was doing here.

The old man kept going on about the noise, and how it was worse at dinner time, and visiting time, and at night time. Basically from what he was saying all the time. I just nodded. I started talking to all of these people but somehow I started to call them names from people in my past or who were in my life now? It was so very strange; it was like they took on the roles for me. The old man I would call dad and the lady that smoked, I would call mum. The nurse with the dark hair, I would refer to her as carol, Marks mum, and the young lad who kicked the ball I would call Paul, as he reminded me of my older brother.

When I spoke to them I actually believed it was them, I couldn't't seem to make the distinction between the two. I must have looked a sight I hadn't washed I smelt of BO, and my eyes had lost all their sparkle I didn't't even recognize myself when I looked in the mirror. At last visiting times! Mark was coming, and soon I would be out of here and I could go home to my baby.

There was a nurse called Keith, he was much older than me, and worked with Marks aunty Gaynor who was a mental health nurse, in a different hospital at one time, but they still spoke and kept in touch. When I found this out, I began shouting out loud that Gaynor was having an affair with Keith. She of course wasn't she was happily married to Gary and her 3 lovely kids. This didn't' go down too well and when I didn't' get the response I wanted from this, I began saying Gaynor was evil and needed to be shot! Which Mark was very upset about.

Mark gave me a huge bag of silver coins full of ten pence pieces, I didn't't realize at the time but it would be the first of many bags of coins to come, for the phone boxes for me over the many months. I rang Gaynor and instead of telling her she was evil and that she was having an affair, I told her how much I loved her down the phone, and that I wanted her to come see me. I wasn't making any sense at all. Mark came with the baby today and she had a little hat on with little booties that I don't remember buying for her, she looked so cute and pink and when Mark went to give her to me, I said; "what are you doing"? "Where's my baby"? "This is a lovely baby but it's not my baby, I have a little boy called jack, where is he"? Mark began to cry and put Ellie back in her car seat. Ellie began to cry and cry, she was only days old and wanted her mummy but I didn't't recognize her as my baby, I didn't't have any urge to pick her up? But I was desperately asking for a baby that I didn't have? They were both crying now, at the same time and then so did I. The three of us should have been sitting at home surrounded by balloons and teddies, and flowers from family and friends, with me holding my precious beautiful little girl with Mark making cups of tea, deciding on who she looked like the most.

Instead we were in a cold room with no windows with the door shut, all looking at each other like strangers crying all in unison we were all in pain. Looking back I don't know if anybody talked to Mark, or gave him any advice and counseling? Or his family, this was all so surreal and nobody that I was connected too had ever experienced anything like this before. I just remember lots of tears and not really understanding why everyone was so upset? I didn't realize that they were crying for me. Or the lack of me, I just wasn't there like an empty shell that looked a lot like me, but wasn't me in any other way.

I don't remember Mark leaving, but I remember waking up I had fallen asleep on my bed, it was night time but not too late about 9pm, visiting time was at 6, I must have slept for a long time. It was dark outside and I woke to people shouting, and crying. There were two people arguing over cigarettes, someone saying that they had been robbed, a man of about 40 wearing a dirty tracksuit, and a woman sobbing saying she hadn't taken them. I woke up on a white bed with the door shut. And had this urge to cry and the urge to scream, I suddenly felt like I was trapped or I was suffocating, and I had to get out. I began to cry and bang on the door, I could look out of the big heavy door and see people walking past but nobody seemed to notice me banging, that made it worse like I wasn't really there, like I almost didn't't exist.

Eventually someone came and I kicked and punched them as hard as I could for ignoring me. I immediately was strapped to the bed and, lots of faces peered around me, I remember feeling frightened wondering what was going to happen next, then the faces started to blur then it went black. I had lots of days like this, and along the way I forgot what day it was, and where I was. It was like I didn't't exist anymore. Whilst all of this was going on, I didn't't realize that my family were desperately trying to get me into a mother and baby unit, were they specialized in what I had.

It was confirmed that I had puerperal psychosis. A severe form of post natal depression. It turned out that there was a mother and baby unit in 60 miles from the one in Merseyside that had some space available but was hard to get a bed. There was a wait of a few weeks but in the meantime I was to be transferred to another ward in a nearby hospital closer to home, a near by Psychiatric Unit. My family had arranged it for me to go, and to try to get better.

Ellie couldn't' come until the mother and baby unit was available, but with the new ward, she could visit with Mark much more often, and it was set up like a hotel, and not a hospital. It was much cleaner, friendlier, and had more staff than the ward in me was in now. For a few weeks it was to be home.

Chapter 9

WINNING THE LOTTERY

I arrived with Mark and my family, and I walked around the place saying hello to people as I did. It had a living room with a huge telly, with big comfy sofas, and an office attached with a door on saying 'staff only'. I remember looking at it thinking it looked odd in a living room, having a door with an office with lots of glass and a sign saying staff only, like you would see in a school.

There were lots of bedrooms attached to it, and two big bathrooms. It was carpeted and warm and had flowery chintz wallpaper on the walls, it was like someone's house except bigger, and it smelt of disinfectant. I put my bags in my room and sat on the sofa and suddenly felt very tired. I put my feet up, and it was just like what I would do at home.

Family came and family went, and all I wanted to do was sleep. I woke up to Ruth the ward manager asking me if I would like a cup of tea. There were lots of people, 'inmates' I would refer to them as. They looked completely normal like you or me, or the staff. It was so hard to imagine them being here because they couldn't't cope with the world, because they needed to get better. There were men and women all different characters. There was a lady who looked quite old with long tatty dyed hair Julie was her name, who was always dressed to the nines wearing clothes that made her look really cheap. She looked like she was about to go clubbing but was 20 years too late. Her face was full of make up and she smoked a lot. She was often abusive and swore all the time at everyone, but for some reason she was nice to me.

Then there was Harry, he was old and grey and had thick rimmed glasses. He would rock backwards and forwards, and would mutter things under his breath. There was Neil, who wore nice shirts and always wore way too much aftershave, he had a clipboard and would mark things down the staff did, and what they had said to him. There were two other young girls like me, Clare would shut herself away, and we could hear her cry herself to sleep in her room. When she wasn't crying she was quiet.

Then there was Dawn she would shout at the top of her voice, and if you looked at her she would tell you to stop, and if you didn't't she would smack you into the middle of next week. There were other people and some names I forget, but these were the ones that stood out for me when I was there.

We were all there for the same reasons to get help and to get better. Everyday we would have group, and talk things through and what was bothering us or upsetting us that day, everybody would have a turn and if there was someone new they would be introduced to the group. Today it was to be my first day.

I realized quickly that, the place had a strict routine, a routine to get up, have breakfast, dinner, and tea. Visiting times and when we had to go to bed. The whole place was run like an army camp.

Ruth was the nurse manager she was kind but to the point, there seemed to be people coming and going, and it was more like a busy house than a ward or a hospital. I was introduced to everybody and everyone was friendly, and would say hello. I remember Julie in her short skirt lighting up a fag, and standing next to the wall, almost as if she was about to go somewhere, saying 'don't worry love you'll be out here soon' she always seemed quite funny to me, a bit of a rebel, and I wondered what had happened to her for her to be in here.

I spent most days in a daze, the days would seem very long, and I would spend time scribbling on pieces of paper, about going home over and over again, or I would watch MTV, or read. But whilst I was doing all of these things, I wasn't me, and it's like I wasn't doing anything and like I wasn't even there. I would switch off and just sit and look out of the window. I looked completely out of it, and if I wasn't in a haze I was asleep. My mum and dad would speak regularly to the doctors and they talked about my medication and changing the dose or trying something else, I was so doped up I didn't't really know what was going on. I knew that at 10, o clock everyday it was morning visits, and it meant Mark and Ellie coming to see me, I would be so excited about being able to see them I couldn't't contain myself. I remember 9.30 seeming like an eternity to get to 10am.

There was a big steel door with a square plate of thick glass that you could see out of and that would be the main door that kept me, us the nutters locked from the rest of the world. It would be double locked, and there would always be someone close by when visitors were coming in and visitors going out. I would say nearly every day at visiting time, someone would try to get out or leave with a visitor. I remember on one of the visiting days Julie got all dressed up as she said some man was coming to see her at visiting time. She had thick make up on, and did her hair, and had the shortest dress on I have ever seen. Seemed strange seeing her all done up like that and she couldn't't go anywhere, but I suppose looking back it kept her sane and kept her feeling some what normal.

On this particular day I was sitting in my pajamas cuddled up to a huge pillow watching her. I was not having visitors till the afternoon, and she was expecting a gentleman friend to come at 10. He never arrived, she waited and waited and he still wasn't there by the time visiting time was over. I felt for her, because when you're in those places it's the visits that remind you of the person you were, and keep you going.

She kept shouting saying; "he will be here" "he said he would"! She said to one of the staff; "don't you dare lock that door"! "He will be here soon", "he will he will"! The last visitor was going out of the door, and she bolted for it. The male nurse who was much bigger than she was, stood in front of it, and he was much too big and too strong for her to move. She started hitting him, screaming and crying, and she was carried off in the air by other staff. Everybody was silent and just stared. Then it went quiet. She had been given an injection and was put in her room.

Over the next couple of days, she didn't't eat or talk. She would ask for cigarettes, and stay in her room most of the time. Then suddenly she would appear as if nothing had happened cracking dirty jokes, and being larger than life, face full of make up, mutton dressed as lamb. I think underneath she was as sick and as fragile as the rest of us. It happened a lot with different people, and I always imagined I would never react like that, and then one day it was my turn.

Mark came with Ellie and visiting time was 45 minutes long. I could see him coming through the door holding her in her car seat.

Every time I saw her she looked so big and cute like a different baby. I would see her face and curl her fingers around my finger and she would look up and beam at me. She was so beautiful; it was so hard to imagine now that she had been inside me, this beautiful little thing.

She always wore clothes that I had not bought or picked out for her, and I asked Mark; "why don't you put the things on her that I had bought when I was pregnant"? I wanted to see her in things that I had picked especially for her, and he said that she had wore them but had grown out of them. She was changing before my very eyes and so fast, and I was missing out on so much. I picked her up out of her car seat and Mark asked me to leave her there for a while as he had just given her a bottle and she may be sick. I didn't care I had not seen her and I desperately wanted to pick her up and hold her. He seemed to get really cross, so I did as I was told and waited. It didn't feel normal, I felt like I couldn't even hold my own baby. I wasn't in control of anything not even my own life. I began to sob.

Mark looked exhausted I think he had grown used to the tears, and seemed to be able to shrug them off. He asked if I was okay, and touched my arm. It was nice to be touched and I swung my arms around him, just like I used to do. He looked uncomfortable and said that I needed to brush my teeth. He was right , I stank, I didn't wash properly, or clean myself the way that I should have been, but it didn't seem to matter in there, it didn't seem to be a problem, but it was. I was Monica the clean freak, this person I had become wasn't me. Looking back I feel I should have had more help with personal care, or encouraged more to be clean, but if I was aggressive and violent towards staff I suppose that was more of a priority, keeping me calm. Not a risk to others or myself. I let go of Mark, embarrassed and then Ellie began to cry. I unclipped her and picked her up immediately, I snuggled her in and gave her, her dummy and she stopped instantly.

It was lovely, I didn't want to let go of her. But I had to, the visit was over, the time had gone and it was time for them to leave. My heart ached and the tears rolled down my face, and I couldn't stop them. His jacket was on, and Ellie was getting clipped back in to her car seat, I felt a rise of panic in me ,I needed my family I needed my baby I wanted Mark, I wanted to be with them right now, not tomorrow.

As they were heading out of the door, I ran towards it and tried to stand in the way, Mark asked me to stop and to let go of his arm as he had to leave with Ellie. I started to shout and cry and stand in the way. The Nurse at the door, pushed me to one side and held me back, and said to Mark, "go". He looked back, and I cried shouting; "I love you", "I love you both". I started to shout and scream and stumbled on to the carpet. When the staff tried to comfort me, I started to hit out. I was taken to my room and told I would feel better after taking my medication. I spat them out, and swore at the nurses. They ended up giving me an injection and I remember falling asleep in my room.

There were other times when visitors would come on this particular day my mum and dad came, my mum said I was talkative, and we spoke about general things and how Ellie was doing etc. The staff made coffee and we sat together in the family room. I was still on heavy medication and this kept me calmer. Visiting time had come to an end and mum and dad got up to leave, there was the usual nurse on the door, I clung to my dad and mum, crying and screaming I wanted to go home with them. The only way that they could pacify me so they could go, was by telling me that they were going to get Mark and Ellie. This was a lie, but it was the only way they could get me to let go.

I clung to the door frame watching them go, banging on the window, watching them leave in the car park, shouting; "don't leave" "don't leave", My mum and dad crying as they left.

In all the visits that I had, everyone carried the same little money bag for me. Either filled with 10's or 20ps, Filled to the top, £5 and sometimes £10 at a time. These were used on the phone daily. I would spend most of my time ringing Mark asking how he was and how Ellie was doing and the money would disappear.

My Mum told me later on of incidents at visiting time, some I can recall and others it's like talking about someone else. My Mum and Dad would visit everyday, on one visit I started telling them and everyone in the room, that I had been raped the previous night. My Mum and everyone that heard me say this on visits were worried if it could happen, but I kept saying it over and over, in both hospitals. On one occasion My mum and dad came to visit me and there were nurses present in the dining room, I would point at a nurse and say; "he raped me last night" The nurse would just look away and not comment. My mum would go around apologizing for me.

One time, my eldest sister Beryl came to visit me. She sat at the table with me, and on lots of occasions we could have our meals when visitors were there. I wouldn't't eat most of the time, and Beryl would try and encourage me to eat my dinner. "Mmm it looks lovely" she would say, and try some. I would point someone out and say to Beryl; "he raped me last night", and "I wouldn't't eat the peas because he wanks in them". Beryl was about to put a spoonful of peas in her mouth, and then changed her mind.

Television was a big part of the night time and we would watch all the usual programmes, the bill casualty and one night the national lottery was on. The numbers were coming out and were displayed on the screen. I obviously hadn't been out and bought a ticket, but as the numbers were coming out, I screamed saying; "these are my numbers "and that "id won the lottery"! I ran around the room saying; "I have won" "I have won"! I went around saying I was going to buy people houses and cars and holidays etc, and there was an Argos catalogue on the coffee table and I began picking things out that I wanted, that I was going to buy with my winnings. The nurse manager asked me what all the commotion was about and I told her. She simply smiled and said, you haven't bought a ticket my love, but keep your fingers crossed for next time.

The days seem to slide into one another and one day could be the same as the next, nothing really changed. There would be always someone to kick off get upset cry or there would be silence that seemed almost deafening at times. I didn't't really know where I was or what I was doing most of the time; I was so doped up I was like a zombie. All I knew about my medication was that it kept me calm, made me very sleepy, and I had to take them twice a day. Family would come and family would go most of the time in tears, my mum said it was like visiting someone else, and Grace was not there anymore. It was like someone had got my brain shook it up and all the bits that fell back down were in the wrong boxes, nothing seemed to make sense anymore.

All in all I had spent 4 weeks there, and I was told the long awaited place my mum and dad had been praying for, and desperately trying to get had came. The day came when I was told that a bed at the mother and baby unit was available. It wasn't a complete mother & baby unit, where there were just mums and their babies there were two beds that had private rooms with cots, and the main Psychiatric ward attached to it. Mum and dad ideally wanted me to be in just a mother and baby unit and not be around other people with problems, as they thought I was too young to be around that, they didn't want that for me. But places were limited and there was nowhere else available. Beggars couldn't be choosers. They looked at it like the road to my recovery. I would finally be in a place where they understood my condition; there were people who could help me, who knew more than what they did and this gave them a lot of comfort. I couldn't wait to tell Mark.

Everybody seemed so excited about this and Mum and dad were told that this would be the steps of my recovery. Mark wanted to drive me there with Ellie, but he was told he couldn't't because I was still classed as high risk and was still sectioned under the mental health act. They had full responsibility for me. So I would have to be taken by them. I packed my things up, I didn't't have much a dirty nightie and some pajamas' and a few warm sets of clothes and some scraggy trainers. Looking back I must have looked a wreck. There was a problem with who was going to take me, and for some reason, I left the ward in a black taxi with Ruth the ward manager.

Chapter 10

THE MOTHER AND BABY UNIT

Mark was following behind with Ellie; I turned around and waved at him smiling through the back window. It was like we were going on holiday, or going on some sort of adventure. The reality was I was a sectioned patient too ill to look after my baby being escorted to a mother and baby psychiatric unit. I got to the huge hospital, and we seemed to be walking around forever trying to find the ward I was going to be placed in, this time with Ellie. We eventually found it ward 21A. I walked through and there was a huge reception desk, with a pretty girl sitting behind it, talking on the phone. It was busy and people were coming and going. Then a Nurse called Bernie came over and introduced herself, and she showed me to my room. As I walked toward the door, there was a little blackboard in the corner with "bay 2" and grace and Ellie written in the top corner.

There was a big window panel in the middle of the door which went right to the bottom, so I could see out but more importantly so they could see in. There were lots of these bays and next door to me was a girl called Claire, and she had a baby too, he was called Harry. I found out later on we got talking that she tried to smother her baby and threatened to kill her fiancé. She had cuts and scars allover her arms. She was very quiet but smiled when she saw me.

As you entered my room, it had a bed in the corner a small modest bedside cabinet, and small wardrobe. Next to the bed there was a cot, beautiful, white with teddies painted allover it. With bedding and a teddy in the corner of it. There was a window in the far corner and out of it you could see the trees. To the left of the room, was a doorway with a kitchen and a bathroom. I didn't't realize that the kitchen was to be shared with the girl next door to me. She had a door like me by where my cot was for Ellie and her cot was for Harry, and when we opened it, we could see in to each others rooms, and we would have access to the kitchen.

Mark put his arms around me and said that I would soon be out of here and that I would be well enough soon to be able to have a day visit. He had all of Ellie's things packed and ready. Bottles bottle warmer, sterilizer, nappies, dummies, and of course Ellie.

He handed her to me, and he looked nervous leaving her with me, he would call her 'stink' and 'Spud' and make a face and she would smile. She was still so tiny. She would have been now 3 and half months old. I held her in my arms and snuggled her soft skin to me, she would just sit there and gaze at me.

Nurses popped in, Claire, and Sarah, they were young but a bit older than me and were very friendly and supportive but in a non condescending way. Even though I had to be monitored and watched, they always apologized before hand and treated me with respect Family came, Mum, Dad and Sue. The nurse asked them all to leave, so I and Ellie could get acquainted with one another and our new surroundings. Mark kissed her head and then kissed mine, he said he would phone me the next day and see me at visiting time. Bernie explained that the nurses would help me with Ellie, and that I was't on my own, and if I needed anything to press the buzzer by my bed.

She explained how the ward worked. She told I when breakfast was, and dinner and tea etc, and that I could go for a walk outside with a nurse or when I had visitors. She showed me where the laundry room was and that I could wash and iron my clothes when they got dirty. There was so much information, I felt tired and so did Ellie, I put her down for a sleep in her new cot and covered her with a blanket I had bought when I was pregnant with her. I felt like I was in control, she was my baby and she was here with me. I lay on top of the bed and Bernie left us to it. Ellie was fast asleep and before long I was too.

I awoke to Ellie crying loudly, I immediately got up and went to her and then she stopped, I looked at the clock, we had been here a while now and she was probably hungry, I picked her up and I could feel that her nappy was full, she was wet through. I suddenly realized I didn't't know what to do? Id always had someone to do this for me, id never done it by myself before. I started to panic and said to Ellie "okay baby ill make it better". I didn't know how to be with her, she was my little baby girl, and she was like an alien to me. I stripped her off and as I did so she just glared at me, looking right into my eyes, she was beautiful, with full red lips and gorgeous blue eyes, it was like looking at her for the first time allover again. I found some clean warm clothes in the bag that mark had left, and changed her, with a clean nappy. I found the poppers on the vest really tricky and got frustrated and shouted for them to pop into place, and as I did I must have scared Ellie because she started to cry. I picked her up and put her against me, and shushed her, and she stopped crying, "I can do this" "I can do this" I kept saying out loud to myself. I found a bottle in the fridge and warmed it. I checked it wasn't too hot, and sat her on my lap and cradled her into me as she guzzled it down. I couldn't help but smile looking at her, her eye lashes were so tiny and perfect, and her little fingers clutched my thumb as she greedily drank her bottle.

One of the nurses came in to see how we were. She seemed pleased I had hold of Ellie and was feeding her. I said "look I am feeding her all by myself". "That's a really good start grace" she said. After I fed her she started to cry and whatever I did to make it better it didn't seem to do the trick. I was tired and wanted to lie down, it was hard work, and I got frustrated and became impatient quite quickly, and pressed my buzzer. A nurse came almost immediately. She took Ellie from me, and sat with me in our room, she figured out that Ellie had colic and had trapped wind from being fed. "she needs to be winded" she said and she rubbed Ellie's back as if to show me. She passed her back to me and I made lots of circular movements on her back and sure enough it worked, she started to burp, and stopped crying.

She was really good most of the time, looking back she was a brilliant baby considering she was passed form pillar to post. She hardly cried but when she did, she sure had a set of lungs on her! She would cry mostly when she wanted to be played with or was hungry and at night, if her bum needed changing she would cry then too. The tablets I had to take made me very drowsy most of the time, I was a walking zombie. So at night when Ellie would cry for me, it was hard for me to wake up, but of course babies wake up in the night, its natural, she wanted me and no one else would do. She would scream at maybe 2 and 3 in the morning, because she needed a bottle or her nappy would have to be changed. I would try and soothe her back to sleep, and sometimes it would work, and other nights it didn't't, she was hungry or dirty and needed me to sort it. I would try and sort it, then at times I would ring the buzzer, and a nurse would come and say "come on grace you need to start looking after your baby now you do it" I would be left holding her wondering where all the help had gone. Looking back with the medication I was taking I think the staff should have done the night feeds and left me to the day feeds, I think that this was wrong. Even though I think the staff wanted me to take responsibility and care for her as this is what I would be doing when I eventually went home, it shouldn't have started as soon as it did.

I would feed her, and my arm would ache, my muscles would be stiff due to some of the medication I was on, and staying in one position for too long was torture. But Ellie could only drink her bottle so fast, I would hold her and scream, and ring the buzzer with tears down my face, and say; "please come and take her" "please take her", sometimes they could see how distressed I was and take her from me, and other times they would watch me but say, "you do it grace" so I had to just get on with it. There help became less and less, but they were always there through the glass looking at me. Sometimes she would fall asleep in my arms and id put her back down and she would wake up, and this could go on for hours.

At 7 in the morning regardless of whatever time I had eventually got to sleep, I would have to get up, and start looking after my baby. There help became more limited, and instead they would suggest ways to help me calm her down when she cried. But make me do it for myself. Looking back I can see that they wanted me to bond with her and do this for myself, and it was part of the process of getting better, as eventually I would get better and would have to do it for myself but I still think the way that it was went about could have been better. They could have gradually supported me at the beginning and then when I was strong enough and more alert, then should have been the time to leave me to it. Some nights I would feel the pressure and say; "take her" "take her" "please I can't do this", and when it got too much they would.

One night she was cutting some teeth, and she desperately wanted her mum, but I just couldn't't look after her, all the staff took turns in taking her and trying their best but it wasn't enough. I went through a stage of not wanting anyone to touch Ellie, but if I wasn't doing what needed to be done, how could it get done if I didn't't want anybody to touch her? When Mark visited he would make up bottles for me to last the whole day and through the night. I would smell the bottles and was convinced they were poisoned, and someone was trying to harm my baby, I would smell the milk, and baby milk has a distinctive smell, different from normal milk,

I would sniff it, and then pour it away. One by One all the bottles would be emptied down the sink, they kept getting made, and I would still pour them away convinced someone was out to harm us.

The nurses and Mark gave up trying to make the feeds and she had ready made bought bottles of milk and I let her have those convinced that they were okay and safe. But after a while, they were not enough to feed a growing hungry baby and she needed that follow on milk to give her all the nutrients and minerals she needed for growth. I immediately on seeing the made bottles threw them against the wall and begged Mark to believe me that they were trying to poison her. He would try and grab the bottles from my hand, and tell me I was being silly and to stop it. But I wouldn't't listen, I was too sick to know any better, and he was too young to realize. Looking back he was 22 years old, and couldn't understand what was happening to his girlfriend? There were meetings of support and information to help him process what was happening and how to help. But every time a meeting or a chat with the doctor was set up, he wouldn't turn up. I don't think he wanted to face that there was a problem, and deciding on rather facing it, he wanted to run away.

One of the nurse managers came in to see Ellie while I was on the phone, I walked in on her, stroking her cheek, I walked up to her and punched her in the nose, the blood poured down her face, and allover her white coat. She stumbled on to the floor, and I hurled abuse at her, in front of Ellie, she began to scream, then all hell let loose.

I was strapped to a bed and all the nurses climbed on top of me and told me to be still. Bernie, the ward manager had big glasses, they reminded me of Deirdre's from Coronation Street, I remember yanking them off her face and telling her to "Fuckoff". There was another time when Mark came to visit and I had been trying to breast feed Ellie, I had no milk left, it had all dried up, and Ellie was desperately sucking at my nipple hungrily for milk, but there was none. Mark was completely taken back by this and demanded to know what the hell I was doing? In my mind at the time, I was trying to care for my baby, and feed her and bond with her. But again, I was all confused and it was the wrong thing to do.

I remember waking up and Ellie wasn't in her cot. In the end the staff realized that I wasn't coping, and they needed to reassess my medication as I didn't seem to be getting better. Eventually Mark came and took her, I remember waking up after they had injected me and looking to see if she was okay, to a ready made cot with no Ellie in it. I was sick, and couldn't look after her properly, but all my maternal instincts were still there.

I touched her cotton sheets were she had been laying, and cradled her bunny, all I longed for when she was here was for her to be quiet, and it was quiet, but it was all wrong, and somehow the quietness seemed deafening. I cried myself to sleep. My Mum and Dad would visit most days, and my brothers and sisters would visit too, but not often. They found it too upsetting, the staff reassured them that I would eventually get better and be 'Grace' again but I would say something inappropriate, or act aggressively. Or generally be lots of things that I wasn't. They would often go home in floods of tears. At the time I wondered what was wrong, and why everyone was crying, I didn't't't realize they were crying for Me., crying for the person that was broken and no longer there.

Chapter 11

Fishing

My medication was changing and getting smaller in dose with some types and bigger in others. At the time I didn't realize what I was on, why I was on them, and what they were doing to my body. One type was diazepam. This was to relax my mood, and keep me in a sedated state. I was either asleep or a walking zombie. I was on others but one type of medication that I was on sometimes affected the other. I remember walking around the ward unable to sit still I had to keep moving. I would spend an hour maybe two walking around the empty canteen in circles; it was like my muscles needed to move. The unit was a psychiatric ward, with beds coming off it, that was them main part of the ward. The only difference to this ward was that there were two rooms designed to keep two mothers and two babies at any one time.

So naturally I would see lots of other people with different problems walking around.

There was a man in the ward called Nick; he was a very tall skinny quiet man. I remember him asking me if I was okay and bringing me tea. He didn't't say much but when he did he talked about fishing. I remember one afternoon, when I had no visitors we pretended in the social room (comfy sofas boards games and books) that we were fishing on a river bank, I was tying bait to the hook, and he was waiting for the fish and telling me the types we could catch and the best places to find them. He would yank his arm back as if he was really getting the fishing rod line into the river, when really we were staring at a grey holy carpet on the floor. Looking back it seems madness that we did this and I find it quite funny, but at the same time, it kept us sane and made us remember who we were.

We got on well, and we would drink tea and chat, he tried to teach me how to play chess, and to this day I still cannot play chess. The day came when he was allowed home, he bought Ellie a brown teddy bear with a big red bow on it for me for when I got her back and said his goodbyes. He was much older than me; early 40's I was a mere 22. When he came to say goodbye I tried to touch him inappropriately, he shrugged me off and told me not to do those things, and kissed me on my forehead.

It was only later I learnt that he had lost his wife and son in childbirth, and had a complete mental breakdown. I think it was wrong looking back that he was on a ward where babies could possibly be, it must have been hard for him. But at the same time people who needed wards could only go were there was space.

Visits were either all at once or not at all, my mum and dad were there every morning but half the time I didn't realize who was there or who wasn't. My sister Tracey had two small boys, she was a single parent and couldn't drive, from her house in Liverpool, to get to Crewe, she needed to get two trains, it took a few hours to get there by train and with two kids in tow, and it must have been hard. She turned up to see me, and the first thing I said to her, after weeks of not seeing her, was; "what are you doing here"? And to "Fuckoff and take your kids with you". She bolted for the door in floods of tears. My mum took her to the canteen, for a cupper and to calm her down, and to explain it wasn't me, and I didn't mean what I had said. My mum asked her to try again. She did, but it was no good, as soon as I saw her I threatened to hit her. My mum suggested maybe another time to come and see me would be better. So she left, 3 hours of a journey and two taxis all for ten minutes of abuse form me.

She tried again the following weekend, it had been

Explained that I wasn't washing, or cleaning myself properly, and to be brutal, I stunk. Anybody that knows me knows how clean I am, and this person, this unclean person that I had become wasn't me. She turned up with a complete dove set, shower gel, shampoo, conditioner body lotion exfoliate cream, the works. I thanked her by throwing the full heavy tubs at her face and screamed at the top of my lungs for her to leave me alone. My sisters decided to try to help with the hygiene side, as the staff just got abuse from me when it was mentioned.

She didn't try to visit me for a while.

Mum and dad would be there every morning to visit me early some days I would cry and sit on them like I was 3, other times I would rant and rave and not make sense, or at other times I would sit in silence. Looking back it must have been so hard for them to see me like this. I was independent and strong willed, it was like Grace had disappeared mum said months later. Nobody seemed to know what to do, except trust in the doctors that I would one day get better, and of course make endless cups of tea.

Mark would visit and bring Ellie to see me, and his visits seemed to shorten, even before visiting was over, but in the mother and baby unit, partners and close family could stay for hours at a time. When I saw her, I would hold her and touch her skin, and breathe her in, her baby smell, and look at the clothes she was wearing, that I hadn't picked out for her, and I would just sit and look at her, I wanted her so much, but I was all mixed up, and didn't know how to show her I loved her, I didn't know how to hold her, or make her feel better when she cried.

I felt awkward with my own daughter. She looked so big, every time I saw her; she was like someone else's baby not mine. It felt like the bond between us was barely there, it was hanging by a thread. One thing that she always did though, when I picked her up, she would stop crying or gurgling, and she would sit and stare into my eyes and smile, she let me know in her own way she knew who I was, and how important I was to her, and at the time, I didn't think it mattered but months later it really did matter that she knew who I was.

This little person, who was apart of me that I didn't know.

The days past, and they all seemed to roll into one another, it was like a haze, and I would spend hours listening to the clock tick and just stare out of the window. In the activity room There was an old rocking chair, it was battered and people had scrawled their name on it, really it wasn't fir for the scrap heap, let alone sitting on, I would sit and rock on it, and think about how I ended up here, and hours would pass, I seemed to forget time, and it seemed to forget me.

Ellie's visits would get longer, and sometimes she would spend the night with me, I would look at her and watch her sleep, and wonder what she would be dreaming about. I would try and make her bottles up, but my hands would get stiff, and I would make any excuse to sit down. I seemed to get tired very quickly. I wasn't getting any better, I was calmer because of the drugs, but I was a walking zombie, my mum would cry, when she saw me, and so would Dave and Carol, Marks mum and dad. Dave would walk out and I would hang on to him like a monkey. Every time I saw him, he had tears in his eyes, and would never look at me directly. Carol would do my hair, she would wash it, and dry it and style it, and try to make it look nice and clean. She would try and chat to me like she used to when I would be getting ready to go out on a date with Mark. Except it wasn't a date, I was confined to the hospital and could hardly remember my own name.

She would try and chat, one day she came to help me wash, and do my hair, and I would say that Mark was better off without me, and that we should split up while I was ill, she would tell me not to be so silly, and that I have to remember how much I loved Mark and what we had. I agreed but it was like a light had been turned off in me. Mark was the love of my life, and to hear me talking like this, it was plain to see to everyone that I was desperately ill.

Brothers and sisters would come and visit, with their hubbies and partners, and all would leave with the same look on their face, and in floods of tears. My sister Beryl and her husband Keith came to see me, Keith was a man's man I had known him since I was 5, he never really said much, I didn't realize how much he loved me or thought of me, but he would sit and listen to me rant on with tears rolling down his cheeks sobbing as I spoke. In all the years I had known him I had never seen him cry. He never came to visit me again.

The order of things was the same, people would come and go, but the person that I wanted to stay with me as much as he could was my Mark. I would see the other girl, in the other room opposite, and her fiancé would visit all the time, and he would sit with her for hours just holding her, and helped with the baby. I would look when the door were open and peek in, and watch them. You could see even though she was ill, and going through the worst time of her life, how in love they were. I ached for Mark, and for him to touch me. I was expecting a visit; I decided to make myself look good. I asked Claire the nurse to help me, she hugged me and said she would do my hair, she gave me lip gloss and smeared some mascara on my lashes, I wore some nice jeans, they didn't fit me, I had lost so much weight, and put a nice top on. She curled my hair, and we sat and talked like two girls going on a night out, not patient and staff nurse.

Ellie wasn't with me, she was with Marks mum, and today he was coming on his own straight from work, I felt excited that I was going to see him, I looked in the mirror, it was me, but it didn't look like me. I waited by the entrance, it was almost half 6, I couldn't wait to put my arms around him. Half 6 came and went, so did half 7, and then half 8. I got undressed, and sat in my nightie, still waiting, no Mark. The nurses came to give me my medication, I said I would have it when Mark visited, they all seemed to look at each other, Bernie said; "Grace I don't think he is coming", I shouted; "he is" "he is" "he is coming, he's just delayed". I sat on the floor, looking down the corridor at the glass that he would walk through, people came in but they were never him. It was nearly 9pm and still no sign. I began to sob, loud sobs, tears streaming down my face, banging my head on the wall behind me. Mark where are you? I need you? Where's my baby? I kept shouting over and over again.

Claire came over to help me up from off the floor, and as she was doing this she was stroking my hair, telling me everything was going to be alright, she handed me a cup, when I got to my feet with my meds in. I lost control, and reacted, and threw the medication against the wall, I cried and cried and cried. This was not my life, I had to get out, I had to go and find my Mark and my Ellie.

I ran toward the door, but before I got there, I was on the floor, surrounded by medical staff bringing a trolley and Bernie telling me to calm down. They gave me an injection, and the next thing I remember was waking up to my Mum and Dad. My Mum stroking my hair. As soon as I felt able I got my coins and went to the telephone box and rang Marks mobile, it rang and rang and no reply came. I then rang Dave his dad he tried to make small talk, and said how he missed me and my naff tea trying to make me laugh. I asked where Mark was, he just said that he was at work, I said; "he never came to see me last night"? And that I had waited, he said that Mark never came home from work, and that he had heard him getting in late, and he took it for granted that he had been to see me.

I started to cry and told him that he hadn't, I sobbed down the phone for all to hear, that I wanted my life back, and that I had to get out of this place, I needed Ellie and I needed Mark.

I couldn't hear anything on the other line other than Dave crying telling me, if he could come and get me he would, but that I had to hang in there. It went quiet then Carol came on the phone, she was crying, and couldn't talk, How's my baby? I would say, she was great, and put the phone to her ear, I could hear her making noises, and I would talk, Carol would come on the phone and tell me how she would smile when I spoke, I wanted my baby, and I needed to go home. I cried so loudly, that the nurses came over and asked me to sit down and have a cup of tea. "I don't want fucking tea" I replied "I want my baby" "I want my lovely boyfriend" "I want my life! "I want my life back".

They had to peel me off the phone, and all I remember was shouting; "Dave come get me" "Dave come get me". The next thing I knew I was drowsy waking up on my bed unable to remember how I got there.

Chapter 12

ECT'

I wasn't getting any better, the medication just seemed to keep me calm when I had my outbursts or sedate me and make me drowsy 24 -7. I really was a walking zombie, it was like I Was there somewhere inside, but very far away, and I didn't seem to know anybody or connect with them, especially my new baby. The doctors had lots of meetings un be known to be with My Mum, Dad, Mark and his parents, all acting on my behalf. It was decided that the medication wasn't making an impact on my condition and that something else had to be done.

I started to lose my appetite, and began to refuse food. The meals would come in silver trays and most of the time, the food wasn't that bad, there would be pizza, jacket potatoes, curry and vegetables etc. But each time the trolley came I would refuse to eat anything. I would drink water and fruit juice, and my body seemed to exist on nothing else. My weight rapidly dropped, and the baby weight that I desperately wanted to lose just after giving birth, began to come off very quickly. My weight was less now than before I was ever pregnant. My clothes didn't fit me, and I would sit in my room when the meals would come. One of the nurses suggested a 'build up shake' they were rich in minerals and vitamins and were meal replacements, they came in chocolate and banana, and I liked them, and for a while it was all I would eat/drink.

The Doctor in charge and the team at the unit decided that they would have to start me on a course of ECT. Electro Convulsive Therapy. It was explained to my Mum and Dad, and then to me that electrodes would be passed through my brain, and would have an impact on the chemical imbalance that was making me behave differently. It was a course of 8 treatments, and the outcome of people having this done was a very good one.

As soon as my Mum heard this, she was horrified and imagined it being like 'one flew over the cuckoo's nest', where Jack Nicholson's character would foam at the mouth, and have a fit on the table. She was against it from the start, not realising it was what I needed to get better and make me Grace again. She demanded that it was not going to happen. But the doctor said that because I was sectioned under the mental health act they could not stop it.

I was over 18, and under their care.

The doctor sat my parents down, and explained that the times had changed over the years and that the procedure was nothing like it was years ago. She explained that it was safe, controlled and I would be supervised whilst under general anaesthetic, and given muscle relaxants, to control my spasms whilst having the procedure. I would be asleep, for all of it, and the whole procedure would be over in half an hour. The doctor explained that there were side effects, and memory loss was one of them. But if it was thought that if the side effects were severe the sessions would be stopped at once.

My Mum took all of this on board. And I was told of what was going to happen to me the following week. I was told I couldn't eat or drink anything apart from sips of water the night before, and I would always have the procedure the following morning. They would always do it in the morning because, I would lose a whole day or most of it, because having it done would be draining for my body, and tire me out completely, or I would suffer a very bad headache, disorientation, and memory loss.

The day of the ECT, I didn't really comprehend what was going to happen, I just did what I was told, and listened to the jargon, I thought it must be really bad or I might not wake up, because My mum and dad were crying outside my room. Before I was wheeled in to the room where the procedure was to be done, my Mum gripped my hand tightly, and said; ''it will all be over soon'', with tears in her eyes, she kissed my head and I kissed her back. I went in to the room, on the trolley bed, with a gown on, and there was a doctor, and a nurse I didn't recognise, and one that I did from my ward. She smiled at me and held out her hand for me to hold it; I nervously reached for it and held it tight.

There was a machine by my bed, with lots of wires and things coming out of it and I remember those putting lots of sticky circles with wires coming off them, against the sides of my forehead, and on my wrist. I was told to lie down, and sit still, at this point, I started to feel a little nervous, and wanted my Mum but she couldn't come in; she had to wait outside, so I gripped the nurse's hand instead. I was told to relax and not to worry and to count from 10 backwards. I remember counting to 8, and then it all going black. When I woke, I had blood on my hand from the needles where the injections had been placed in to my hand. I remember waking up and feeling very woozy and tired, having the worst headache I have ever had. My head ached and I just wanted to sleep.

I woke to my Mums face staring at me, she was still crying, and moving my fringe out my eyes. Dad came over and kissed me on the head. I wanted to sleep, and the nurses urged Mum and Dad not to stay too long. I must have slept the clock round because when I woke, it wasn't morning anymore it was late afternoon. It was visiting time soon, which meant Mark and Ellie coming. That cheered me up. But when visiting time came there had been a phone call, Mark couldn't come because of work, and Ellie was with Carol and Dave. I cried and cried. I would go back to bed, and fall asleep, and forget that they were not coming, and be left disappointed all over again. It was decided that I was to have two ECT Sessions per week. My Mum was told that there would be no change in me from the first session, but in time after a couple there would be a big difference in me. This proved to be true.

After the third session my Mum said it was like she could see me again. She said that instead of a big black void behind my eyes, she could see me coming through. I would greet her and kiss her like before and we could have a normal conversation again, I wasn't completely myself but it was so much better than before. They were pleased there was a difference. Small, but a difference, there was hope. I started to wash myself again and get a bath, something I had to be nagged to do or be helped with before. I would get up and wash my hair and dry it, and get changed in to clean clothes. This was a vast improvement. My mum said it was nice to see me clean. Even Mark noticed when he visited me, and he no longer resisted kissing me because my breath stank, because I hadn't cleaned my teeth. I began to enquire more after Ellie, and all my motherly instincts seemed to come flooding back.

I wanted my baby she should be with me. I urged for this, and not long after she was. Mark brought her in, and seemed nervous that he was leaving her with me, he had had her, and looked after her when he came home from work, and in the day his mum had her. She was glad to go back to work, and Mark would have to leave her with me, her Mum, the way it should have been. The day came when I got her back, she was dressed all in pink so cute, and she gave me the biggest smile I have ever seen, when she saw me.

The tears rolled down my face, Mark had only just taken her out of her car seat, and I already had her in my arms, kissing her and cooing at her, she had grow so big. I couldn't believe how much hair she had. She smiled at me and her eyes darted wherever my face was. She must have missed me as much as I had missed her. This void that wasn't there, being a mum and not knowing how to be one, lacking in feeling, I didn't feel right, but the need to be with her and hold her was so strong, I didn't understand it myself. But all I knew was it felt right when she was with me, and I didn't seem as agitated. The first night was hard, she was teething, she woke in the night, and needed calpol, and bonjella, As soon as she woke, I was up and by the cot, soothing her and talking to her whilst getting whatever she needed. The nurses heard her crying, and came in to the room, they seemed surprised that I was up, and ready to look after her, they came in the room, and they asked if I needed any help? I said no and for them to leave me to look after my baby myself. They Said okay and shut the door.

For the first time since I began this nightmare, I just wanted my privacy and to look after my baby. There was a big long pane of glass in the door, and they had their eyes through the door every ten minutes. Ellie had gone to sleep in my arms, and I was about to put her down, feeling pleased that I had done it by myself, when the nurse walked in to check on me, and woke her up. I went mad and told her to pissoff, at which point she told me to calm down. I shouted just "fuckoff" "and leave me in peace with my baby"! She asked me to remain calm, and the more she did this, the more I wanted to smack her. I saw how upset Ellie was by the noise, and immediately quietened down. Because I was on 15 min observations. They checked on me through the door, all the nurse had to do was look and see that I was getting Ellie off to sleep and once she was in her cot and settled she could have checked on us then? She didn't even need to do that because she could see for herself she was fine and so was I. It was like I had been robbed of everything even my privacy with my baby that you take for granted. I had managed to do one thing right, and she managed to ruin it for me, and I was so angry that this had been taken from me too.

She left and I tried again to make Ellie better, and snuggle her to sleep. Some nights she would be asleep, in my arms, all wrapped up in a soft blanket, all warm and pink.

I would sit and look at her beautiful face, her tiny eyelashes that were so long and perfect, and her curved little lips that moved when she slept. She was so beautiful, and perfect. I would look at her and cry, she didn't deserve all of this, she didn't deserve a Mother that was crazy and didn't know what the hell she was doing, and she deserved to be loved and hugged and tucked in bed every night. I would cry for all my plans that all went wrong, and how she must have suffered, I wanted to be her Mum and love her and be there like all Mums are but I didn't know how, all the emotions and feeling were there, but I didn't know what to do with them. I kept getting the ECT sessions and I started to become more like myself, I talked more, washed and made an effort more, but most of all wanted to care for Ellie more. I was like a robot doing things for her, but it was me that was doing them, not a nurse or Mark, Me. I wanted to do them, but I somehow did them without emotion, I wanted to be her Mum, and change her nappies, and change her clothes, but there was still something missing.

I improved so much over the next few weeks that it was agreed I could have a day visit. I was thrilled; I could leave the hospital with Ellie. I could be normal, at least for a day. My Days would consist of getting up, with difficulty as I would be very tired, even when I had been asleep all night, and I would be the one seeing to Ellie now, not the nurses. I was calmer, and found them watching me intrusive and I would try to ignore it and carry on. The room went from a complete untidy tip to a shiny pin. Everything had its place, and it was cleaned by the cleaners. Before they would be trying to clean around a mess, this wasn't me or the way I lived. When the staff and Mum started to notice this they realised that this visit home was what was needed, I needed to be reminded of how I used to live, and how I used to be. There was a long way to go but I was on the right road. Ellie had been born in February, and that seemed like an age ago. It was the end of April and I could go outside in the real world, and go for a walk and take my baby out in her pram. Something else I had been robbed of. All my plans were not taken, they were just delayed, and this helped me to carry on.

Chapter 13

THE DAY VISITS

I had an interview with the head doctor, to assess me and to make sure I had improved enough to be let out. She asked me how I was feeling and what I wanted to do for my first day out. I said that I couldn't wait to walk my baby in her pram, as I had never done it before. She was 3 months now, and I hadn't even taken her for a walk yet in her lovely pram, you couldn't count the grounds of the hospital.

I said that I wanted to be with Mark and Ellie. She was happy that it was safe, and that I was well enough to leave the hospital, but that I would have to be back by 6pm on the day of the visit. I was thrilled I couldn't wait to get my ten pence's out to rush to the phone to ring Mark. I got hold of his mobile, and the coin box was eating in to the little money that I had left. 'Hi Mark, its Grace' 'guess what'? "I can come home for the day this weekend;

"Isn't that great"? "Grace I am working, all weekend I can't get out of it", "you will have to come out for a day next week instead". He said. I began to cry and before I knew it the tears were streaming down my face. Mark couldn't understand what I was saying anymore. 'Grace calm down, I will be in to see you tonight I promise'; the line went dead. This was the first time I had the opportunity to come out and be normal, and it was like I was the only one who seemed excited about it.

I saw all the same people walking around and playing endless games of chess and cards, and I suddenly wanted to scream. But I stopped myself,

71

maybe I could still have a day out with Ellie. I rang my Mum and she could sense I had been crying, I told her my good news but she had already been told. She said it was great. I explained that Mark had to work, and she said; "don't worry we will sort something out". I had a call from my sister Sue the following hour, she said for my first visit; I could go and spend it with her and Ellie at her house in Liverpool. I was excited.

Mark came like he promised that night, and I practically jumped on him when he arrived. He looked tired, and looked like he just didn't want to be there. He said that I had to stop ringing him so much, as he was busy, and that he would ring in the mornings and at night when he was about to go to bed. I said that I missed him so much and that was why I wanted to ring him all the time. He seemed irritated and I offered to make him a coffee, he said he didn't want one. The door to the kitchen opened and the girl next door came in with her partner, and said hello. Mark said hello back and asked after their baby. He seemed to be able to talk normally with everyone, everyone except me.

He didn't stay long, and when he was leaving, I went to kiss him on the lips and he kissed me on the forehead, and squeezed my hand. I saw him leave, and even though as sick as I was, I knew something had changed in him, and in us. As he left to go to the back door, I raced to him, and he stopped and said 'don't leave Ellie'. I mouthed 'I love you' and 'I will get better' I promise. He smiled and nodded and left.

The very next day was a Saturday and this was the day I would be allowed outside in the normal world. I couldn't wait. My sister Sue turned up with her friend Joanne. I didn't know her very well, but she had been and bought me a really nice bra and knickers set. They looked really nice and new. I thanked her and asked Sue in front of her why she was here? Sue said that she wanted to help her with my visit and that she had bought me something. I had met her lots of times in the past, but when I saw her on this day, I couldn't place her, she looked familiar but that was all. Looking back I don't thin k my sister should have brought Joanne, as good as her intentions were, she was not part of my life or my 'normal' surroundings outside the hospital and that's what I needed. I needed to be reminded of my life and what was important to me not my sisters. But my visit should have been at home, not at my sisters, as this couldn't happen they made the best of what they could arrange. I think my first visit home should have been planned better, and of taken place when Mark wasn't going to be in work. It should have been organised when he was at home and waiting for me to have my visit. I think the communication could have been better.

Joanne seemed to know me and smiled a lot at me. I looked at the Bra and knickers and put them in my cupboard, with all my others, they were all old and grey and tatty, I looked at them and thought, and when I look a bit better I am going to wear them for Mark.

Ellie sat in her car seat, smiling and looking at Sue and her friend. I felt really proud of myself. I had managed to change her nappies all night, and bath her in her baby bath by my bed, just me and her, and the staff looking in the window from time to time. That morning, I bought her a little suit from the shop in the hospital. I gathered all m y money together and walked in. The shop was covered in teddies and booties and balloons, and in the corner were baby clothes. I scanned them thinking they would all be newborn, and as I was doing this the lady came over and could see I was searching for something in particular." have you any 3months plus clothes? For a little girl" I asked. She looked through and even brought out what was in the back. There were dresses and little suits, pinks and reds, beautiful and perfect for Ellie. In the end I chose a pink cotton dress with little flowers all over it, it was beautiful. I was so excited to put this on her I nearly fell over someone getting in the lift to get back to her. I put it on her. It was nice for her to be wearing something that I had picked. Apart from what I bought her when I was pregnant I hadn't bought a single thing or chosen something for my baby, it felt well.

With all the excitement of going to my sisters, and getting Ellie ready all by myself, I forgot to have a shower myself, or brush my teeth. My hair was limp and greasy. I had an old t shirt on and faded jeans that kept falling down, they were maternity ones, I looked a sight. Sue came in with a bag, and inside, there was a new top, and new combat pants and some flat pumps, and a fleece. They were really nice, I hadn't had new clothes or looked nice in so long, I wanted to put them on right away, But sue said; "no, when you come to mine you can have a bath" and be all clean and the wear them". She smiled a big smile, and squeezed my shoulder she held Ellie's car seat and things that she needed for that day. I had Ellie in my arms and we began to walk out of the ward, the nurses were watching and looking at me, and smiling, as if to say 'your getting there grace'.

One of the nurses winked at me and came over, he said, "it won't be long when you're going home for good". I smiled and as I walked down the big long corridor holding Ellie tightly as I did, I began to feel nervous. Suddenly we weren't in the hospital anymore, we were outside and I could feel the warmth of the sun on my back. People were coming and going in and out of the hospital, every body seemed to be in a rush, the world had sort of stood still for me, but the world was carrying on outside for everybody else.

We got to the car, and I felt in a daze. Was this really happening? Could I cope outside? Even though I was desperate to leave, I suddenly realised that I needed the hospital and seemed to slow down the nearer we got to Sue's car. She noticed immediately and hugged me and said; "don't worry" "we are going to have a great day, and then we will drive back to the hospital later".This eased my tension and I was glad that she was with me.

The journey was an hour long, Ellie slept for most of the way, and Sue and Joanne tried to make conversation with me, but I didn't feel like talking, I suddenly felt very tired. I heard them chat about this and that, and I suddenly realised I didn't even have anything to talk about? What could I say? I seemed to forget how to be with other people and my body language was closed. I wanted to hug myself and wake up and be Grace again.

We got to her house, and people came to see me and ask after Ellie, they didn't stay long and I was glad, I felt dizzy with all the visitors. I asked Sue if I could have a lie down on her bed. I went straight upstairs, and clutched the blanket and wrapped it around me. I wanted the world to go away. I felt like I was on a rollercoaster, and I wanted to get off. I didn't want to talk and to laugh, and to sit; I didn't want to be in hospital, but I didn't want to be here either. I felt lost and didn't know what to do with myself. I heard Ellie crying downstairs, hungry for her bottle. I walked downstairs, Sue handed me a cup of tea and I took Ellie from her and gave her, her bottle. She stopped crying, I sat and held her and after a while she fell asleep. I sat on the sofa, and couldn't relax, I didn't know how to sit or act, this was what I wanted, to be out, to be normal, but I felt far from normal, I felt like a prisoner in my own body. I suddenly realised that I shouldn't be here, I should have been at home with Mark and Ellie with all, of my things and Ellie's things, in my life not someone else's. I had an urge to cry, but nothing came out. I felt panicky and my hands were sweating. I thought I would come out and instantly revert to being me again; this was not what happened it just reminded me of how sick I actually was.

The TV was on and I was glad, I could escape my own thoughts, and just sat looking at the TV, I was somehow able to switch off. There was a knock at the door, Michaela, My brothers then, Fiancé came through the door. The last time that I had saw her, I said she was evil, and tried to harm her, I couldn't really remember it as me doing it, I knew it had happened but how it happened and why didn't register in my head. She had her little girl, my niece with her, Taylor. She walked in the room, and smiled as she came in. 'Hello Grace' and she sat down, not too close to me. I said hello back, but just sat there, I didn't feel like talking, I didn't want to see her and be reminded of what I had done or said, I felt uncomfortable. I wanted to sleep. Michaela always wore nice clothes and make up, and today was no exception. She was wearing casual clothes, but smart, with nice shoes and her hair done and make up applied to perfection.

She was pretty, and a little older than me. But to look at me, I looked like an old dirty rag doll. Looking at her I felt old, ugly and like nothing, almost even not a person. Suddenly I really wanted to be clean.

Sue ran me a bath, and filled it with bubbles. I got undressed I was shocked at how long the hairs on my legs were, they were almost two inches long. Black and shiny sticking out of my legs, it just didn't seem important to shave, the hairs under my arms were like a man's armpit, and my toe nails were like talons. All the things that you do to keep yourself clean everyday in the real world we do it all the time, and keep on top of it without even realising it. I just seemed to forget these things.

Sue came in with hot towels, and seemed shocked to see my legs and how hairy and long they were. She handed me a new lady shave out the cupboard and began trying to shave them. But they were too long and kept getting caught in the blade. She sat with me, and one by one we cut them down, as short as we could. I sat in the warm bath, and lay down, it was warm, and I felt safe I didn't want to get out.

Sue asked if I had ever had a bath with Ellie. I said no, and she said that maybe it was time I did. She told me how she had done this with all three of her kids, and how it was nice to get in the bath with your baby, and play with them. She got her undressed and she placed her on top of me. She was all slippery and bubbly, and smiled and cooed. I washed her body and massaged her back and cuddled her in. This is what normal mums do, I thought. Sue kept checking on us, coming in and making up things to ask me, just to check we were both okay and safe, but she gave me privacy, special precious privacy, that's taken for granted and something that I never had with my baby. And for that I will always be grateful. She washed my hair, and dried it, and put cream on my face. I put my new clothes on that she had bought. When I looked in the mirror, I looked different. I looked a little like the girl I used to be before I was ever pregnant. It was nice to see myself in the mirror.

The day flew by, and before I knew it we were back in the car and driving back to the hospital. I fell asleep on the way back, and I never thought I would even think this, but I was glad to get back to the hospital. Sue had bought me some new pyjamas, and when I entered my room, it had been cleaned and new sheets were put on the bed. I couldn't wait to get in it. I was tired. Ellie needed her night clothes and bottle, and before I knew it she was fast asleep in her cot. It had been a busy day; I turned the lights off in my room. And fell fast asleep.

Un is known to me Sue had told them how I had been on the visit, and told them how tired I was, and that it went well. The staff were delighted by this, and the news spread through the family, that this was hopefully the road to getting better.

I kept getting the ECT sessions twice a week, and again each time, I seemed to lose a whole day once the procedure had been done. I would wake with the worst headache I could ever imagine, and would sleep most of the time. But each time I had the sessions, I would get better and better. I took care of myself more, spoke and behaved like a person should. The outbursts and violence became non existent, and most importantly of all, I was caring for Ellie, and wanted too. My mum came in to see me one visit, and she saw me cleaning my room, and sorting washing out for myself and the baby. I was dressed and my hair was washed. Ellie was in her bouncer gurgling happily, and playing with a rattle, and the radio was on. I stopped what I was doing and hugged my Mum, and asked her if she wanted a cup of tea. My Mum began to cry, I asked her what was wrong, and she said 'nothing love' it's so nice to see you like this' you look and sound just like my Grace' your getting better.

I hugged her and we sat and had a drink of tea. If you took the room and the glass doors away, it would have been a normal set up, grandparents coming to see their granddaughter and having a drink. I really was getting better. So much so, it was time for another visit. But this time, I could come home for a whole weekend! I was still nervous but this time I knew it would be with my family. I couldn't wait.

Mark had taken two days off work. I was so excited; I could be in my house with Ellie and Mark. I waited and had me and Ellie ready at 8am. The nurses couldn't believe it, they normally had to wake me and give me a push but not today, I could have a normal family, even if it was just for a weekend. Mark came through the door, and I raced to greet him, he smiled and went straight over to Ellie. ''Grace what is she wearing'' he said? I said, ''A suit I got her, do you like it''? It was too small, I had squeezed her in to a baby grow suit which was tight. He took her little feet out of the legs, and snipped the feet off, and put some socks on her. "I will buy her some new outfits" he said. "I would love to pick them can I go with you"? "No I will buy them on Monday and bring them to the hospital" he said. I agreed and we set off. Ellie strapped in the back and me and Mark in the front. It was like an everyday thing that people do, but it was all new to me. We passed the ice cream factory, every time we set off back home, and when we passed this time, Mark said we will have to go there one day. I felt excited but nervous all at the same time. Mark took a different turn off, as we neared home, 'where are you going' I said you have gone the wrong way home? He said that when I went in to hospital he moved in to his mum's house and that we were going to spend the weekend there. I felt crushed and my chest felt heavy, what I thought was going to be me and him and Ellie didn't happen. I took it for granted that's what would have happened, but I never said and he never asked. I didn't want to be the 'freak' again trying to fit in around other people and their lives, I wanted mine, and it had been so long I had forgotten. It wasn't that I didn't want to see Dave and Carol and Emma, I just wanted to be in my bed and my home, and I was so disappointed. Looking back I wish the communication between us had been better, and that we talked more, and we kept each other informed as to how we felt and what was happening. "Can't we go home to our house"? I said, he said "no".

When we pulled up, Mark's dad Dave was already at the gate ready to greet me, waving madly at the window. As I got out of the car, he had his arms wrapped round me, and tears in his eyes. 'This is the start of things to come woody' he said, he always called me woody, and he kissed me on my head and then gave Ellie a big kiss too. Carol Marks mum, was already working on dinner, and came out with the tea towel on her shoulder, and grabbed Ellie out of the Car seat and instantly started hugging her and kissing her. She kissed me and said she had made my favourite. We went inside and Emma was there with her Boyfriend, she swung her arms around me, and said that she had bought me a lip gloss. She was in her teens, and she looked up to me like a big sister. 'We've all missed you around here' she said.   Her boyfriend being young and not knowing what to say asked if I wanted a cuppa. I said yes.

We ate and got DVD's in and sat around the living room, just like we had done every other weekend since I was a teenager. But this time it was different, I felt like I didn't fit in, and if I fitted in anywhere it was always with Marks family. I felt at home and I felt safe. I loved them as much as mark, and missed them like I missed my own Mum and Dad. Carol completely took over with Ellie, and told me to have a break. I had changed her in to the outfit that was too small. Carol took them off, and produced a NEXT bag from behind the couch; Mark said she needed some new clothes so I have got her some new pretty things. 'Oh' I said. ''I wanted to do that''. ''Its okay my mums done it now'' Mark said; ''you relax''. She changed her, she fed her, she bathed her, I was happy for her to do it, and I was tired and wanted to lay down a lot of the time. But even though I was still sick, I knew something was wrong, and that I should be doing it. She was by Carol's chair, when she was watching TV, and I moved her bouncer toward me, I smiled and stroked her hair and she looked up at me and beamed at me. I smelt she had definitely filled her nappy. I went in to her bag and couldn't find anything, it was empty. Carol had woken up; ''I have bought her a new bag Grace, the old one was getting tatty, all her things are in there''. I got out a nappy and before I could take it back to her, she was already changing her. ''I was going to do that,'' I said. ''Its okay;'' Carol said ''you relax'', ill do it. I wanted to take Ellie from her and run away, to go home, and be in control, but instead I just sat in the kitchen.

Looking back I think they should have been advised. I didn't want ''a break'' I wanted to be with Ellie and got be allowed to be her mum. All of Carol's kindness was there but I was angry and I didn't know what to do with it. I felt left out like the ugly useless lump that had given them a beautiful grandchild and I wasn't needed anymore, I felt lost, I felt alone and I didn't know how to act or what to say.

Dave sensed something was wrong, he came in and asked me what the matter was. I said I was fine. He hugged me, and made me a drink of tea, and went o cut the grass in the garden. Night time came, and Carol, had Ellie all ready for bed, she was in her Moses basket, she was way too big for it really but it would have to do this weekend. Carol said goodnight and said Ellie can sleep with us; you can have a good sleep then. That was it for me; Ellie was my baby and as much as I had appreciated all she had done there was no way I was having anyone tell me what was happening with my child. Sick or not or grandma or no grandma my instincts kicked in and took over. ''No I want Ellie to sleep with me'' in Marks room. I think she sensed I needed to be with her, and that she may have been doing too much from the expression on my face. I and Mark needed to be together with our baby even if she was asleep. She went to bed, and Ellie slept right by the bed next to us, I tucked her in and got in to bed and waited for Mark. I had one of Dave's old shirts on, and being in Marks old room, reminded me of when we were younger, and he would sneak me in, after a night out. Except there were no All Saints and Oasis posters on the walls.

It was getting late and still no sign of Mark. I crept down the stairs, and he was talking quietly on his mobile. "Mark" I whispered and he jumped out of his skin. "I have to go" he said to whoever he was on the phone to and he hung up. 'Who was that' I said. It was work'. 'At this time'? Mark you need a break? All the hours you have done this week and they are still ringing you? Do they know I am out of hospital for a weekend? "Yes" he said. He changed the subject and came up to bed. We were sharing a single, and he complained, but it was nice and reminded me of being 16 again. I put my arms around him, it was so lovely to smell him, and have his lovely eyes looking at me. I wanted to kiss him. I did and he kissed me back. I put my arms around him tightly, and I didn't want to let go. It was the first time in a long time we had been close enough to touch each others skin. I started to kiss him, and he kissed me back, he took off his Dad's shirt, and I wanted to make love to him, it had been so long, I wanted to breathe him in, and feel him next to me. I loved him so much. We started to kiss, and I climbed on top of him, the bed creaked and the head board made a noise, just like it had always did when we were young. "Stop" Mark said. 'I can't grace' "Mum and Dad are probably still awake", "and we will wake Ellie up". He moved away from me, and went o the bathroom. We hadn't touched each other for months. Something was off and wrong, he had never been this way with me before, I felt rejected I wanted to cry, but the tears just wouldn't come out. Instead I lay there and pretended to be asleep. He came back in and said my name. I didn't answer he turned over and went to sleep.

The next day Carol and Dave, were going to their friends for roast dinner, and that id been invited, I didn't want to be with anyone I didn't know well. I didn't want to go. But Ellie was dressed in a peach little dress, with matching head band all ready to go in her car seat. "I am going to take Ellie then if you don't want to come, that okay"? She said as she was walking out the door. Expecting that it was fine as she was heading out. It didn't seem to matter what I wanted anymore from anyone. 'Fine I said'. I kissed her cheek and waved her goodbye. Emma had stayed in her boyfriends and when Dave and Carol had left, it was just me and Mark. I felt uneasy; I was scared of saying something wrong, I couldn't relax. I was twitchy and couldn't sit still, but didn't want to move either. I didn't know what to do with myself. I sat and rocked myself, and bit my fingernails. 'Liverpool's playing in a bit, do you mind if I watch it?' he said. "No", I hated football, there were magazines and things to do, but I couldn't do any of them. I suddenly wanted to be back at the hospital.

We sat and watched the football, and I lay on his lap and he stroked my hair. I felt lost and I felt alone. Carol and Dave came back, and I felt glad to see Ellie. I picked her up and hugged her. The weekend had gone so quick, it was time to leave to get to the hospital for 6pm. We were quiet in the car, and didn't talk much. As we walked down the ward and in to my room, Mark dropped the bags and put Ellie's bottles in the fridge. 'I am going to go grace' he said, it's an hour home, and I am really tired. He kissed me on the cheek and kissed Ellie on her head and left. I started to change Ellie and sort us out for bed time. I felt like I was more in control at the hospital, even though I had eyes on me at all times, I felt like I knew what was expected of me, and what I had to do. In the real world, I didn't know my routine or what I had to do. I felt like I was in limbo. At the time, Carol was just trying to help me, and give me a break, but I had lost so many precious moments with Ellie, and I needed to strengthen that bond. Instead of giving me a break, she should have encouraged me to change Ellie, and feed her, and take her for a walk. I was too ill, to realise this at the time. But hindsight's a marvellous thing. I think looking back the hospital should have spoken to both families and communication being open is so important. Looking back I ache when I read the words on the page because I remember feeling those awful feelings, that could have so easily of been avoided. It should have been planned and clear what was happening and what I would be doing and that I knew before hand. In hospital everything is routine, when you eat when you have visitors, there was even a time slot when you did your washing and when the medication was given. Whilst ill, this routine without realising it helped me so much. I hated it when it was there and I knew nothing else, but when I came out nothing was organised, or done in a routine, and I felt like I couldn't cope. It could have been planned by Mark and his family, and I could have been asked what I wanted, and what I wanted to do, instead of it being the other way around. They had control over what they did and wanted and could do it wherever and whenever they liked. But I didn't, and the time that I did have was two days. It could have been done so much better, but the family could have been informed better, and advice and support outside the hospital should have been clearer.

Chapter 14

MARIA

The weeks passed, quickly, and I knew I was getting better because I wanted to do more, and I was growing tired of the same routine.

When I had visitors, I wouldn't be in bed anymore; I would be up, cleaning my little kitchen, or changing Ellie, or washing clothes in the laundry room. Everybody felt like Grace had come back, in some form.

My Mum regularly rang my best friend Maria, the whole time I was in hospital, I didn't know this, and every time she was mentioned, I would fly in to a rage. But when the time was right, Mum would gradually bring her in to the conversation. "Maria would love to see you" "How do you feel about her coming to see you Grace"? She would say. "I don't want to see anybody right now" would be my answer. But the rages when she was mentioned seemed to stop. Un be known to me, Mum rang her every week and gave her an update on how I was. At first Mum told me Months later when I was home, that Maria would be in floods of tears talking about me. Then gradually Mum would explain how ill I was, and everything that I said and did that day, was not me, and how she had told her to hold on to our friendship, and that I would need her when I eventually came home.

Maria seemed to understand what Mum was telling her, but like everybody else I have spoken to since my illness, what I had, just wasn't heard of, somehow it was really hard to believe that me having a baby could have that effect on my brain. Every week, Mum would ask her if she would like to come and visit me and that she would stay with her whilst she saw me. Every week plans were made, and every week plans were broken. Maria missed me in her life, we shared everything together, we went to school together and we lived around the corner from one another. This was the first time since we were 14 that I was to not have her in my life. I was too sick to notice that I missed her and needed her more now than I ever did before. But there was a void that was there in her life and definitely in mine. We had always been there for each other no matter what, it was the first time I had gone through something, and not had her at my side. Mum stopped asking in the end, but kept ringing to let her know how I was doing. Maria just couldn't face me, her best friend that she knew like the back of her hand. What if I wasn't the same? What if I flew in to a rage? Maria was finding it hard me not being there, but it was easier to put it off than face me and it being totally different. Mum seemed to understand and when the time was right we would hopefully sort it out.

On one particular day, Ellie was asleep in her cot, and I was sitting in my little shared kitchen on my own. I turned the TV on, I hadn't watched a programme or looked at the TV for months, and before I was sick I was a real telly head. My favourite was Eastenders, I never missed it, and I hadn't seen it for months. The familiar music came on, and I hadn't a clue what was going on? There were new characters in it, and I didn't know them, I didn't know what had happened and it upset me. I turned the TV off, and I sat there looking at the blank screen. Everything seemed to have changed for me and I felt like I couldn't keep up. I heard the familiar sound of the swinging door in my room. It was one of the nurses, 'There's a phone call for you Grace; 'who is it'? She didn't answer.

I got to the reception, and I heard "Hi Grace how is you"? "Who is it"? "Its Maria" said the voice. I went silent, I didn't know what to say, I asked how she was, and she asked if I was getting better, she asked after Ellie, and said how big she must be now. She said that my Mum had been ringing and keeping her informed as to how I was. I thanked her for ringing and said that I felt tired and that I needed to lie down. "You do that Grace" she said, "take care". And with that she was gone.

We always chatted for hours when we got on the phone, and would laugh like two silly school girls and go into every single detail of what had happened to us that day. It was the shortest conversation I had ever had with her, and we always said love you at the end of every conversation. It was an ice breaker, and no doubt down to my lovely Mum. My Mum asked if I had any news when she came the following day, I told her that Maria had rang, she seemed very pleased, and shocked almost I didn't realise it was her who had given Maria the number and courage to ring. I would sometimes hug my Mum and plead with her that I was going to get better almost convincing myself. My mum would always say of course; "you are you are going to be fine".

I got a letter through the post too, as well as cards from friends and family. I attached all of these to my wall, and would look at them along with my photographs everyday. The letter I got that day was from Pam, my friend who lived over the road from me. I met her when I had bought my house, the day I moved in. me and Mark had pretty much nothing at all, and it was late when we moved. We contemplated going to the chippy with the measly pounds that we had left. Then there was a knock at the door. It was Pam. She introduced herself, and she brought two casserole dishes across each with two tea towels draped over them. One was a sausage casserole, and the other was a baked cake. That was the first time I had met her, and she was to become a very close friend and still is. She was kind and friendly, and helped me out so much when Ellie was little, a person that would do anything for anyone. I opened up a typed letter from her; it was pages long, which were nice as people who sent letters and cards never really knew what to say, but not Pam. She was the chatterbox of the street! And if anybody could talk the hind leg off a donkey it was lovely Pam.

She told me about her holidays, and what she had been up too, she told me how she had kept an eye on my house and planted lots of plants and put a hanging basket up for me. It seemed strange her talking about my house, and her being there outside of it, and me being here. She asked after Ellie and she said that she had got lots of things for Ellie when I came home. The letter cheered me up no end, and it was nice to hear someone talking about their lives and not feeling sorry for me for a change. I appreciated this letter so much and even then when I didn't know Pam as well as I does now, I appreciated her all the more. I still have that letter and all those cards even today.

The girl next door was leaving with her partner and her baby. It didn't seem fair, and it had a huge impact on me. She gathered all her things up. And seemed happy and in control. She could go home. But I couldn't. Her going seemed to make me want to leave even more. I think this could have been talked about to me, and I could have even of been prepared for it, as it did affect me a lot. The room was empty for a few days, and then one day a new girl with her baby boy came to stay. I could see the terror in her eyes and as she walked around soaking up her new environment, I remember how my first day had felt. It seemed so long ago now. I instantly wanted to help her and make her feel welcome and that she wasn't alone in what had happened to her. I said hello and smiled as softly as I could. But when her partner left all I could hear was her crying. I knocked on the door. She was sobbing on her bed, and her baby had been taken away. She looked up, and she saw me enter her room. I handed her a hanky one of my dads seventies style brown ones; she took it and stopped crying. 'I know you don't think it right now, but you will get your baby back and you will get better. I said, "I know because the exact same thing had happened to me". Everyday I would go and see her, her name was Helen and her baby was Connor. Some days she would want to sit and chat and other days she would lock herself on her room and not talk to anybody. That was fine because I knew what it was like. We just sort of understood how it was, and it wasn't awkward. I felt like we were in the same boat, out to sea without a paddle, and at one time we were both without our beloved babies. Somehow seeing other people like me, or even in the same place as me, it made me feel better, I didn't feel alone I felt like it happened, and it didn't just happen to me. Helping her or at least trying to help her made me feel human again, and like I had battled most of it in a way and it made me feel stronger.

I got better and better, and managed to even have a joke with people. Something I hadn't been able to do for a very long time. I sat in the games room, and struggled to understand Chess, I would attempt to read books, something I loved to do, but I couldn't keep up, I would pick them up, and no sooner they would be down again. I couldn't concentrate or sit still. The visitors seemed to leave happier and hardly anyone cried anymore when they came to see me. The day came when I was told I was to be allowed home.

Chapter 15

COMING HOME

I couldn't believe it, I was finally well enough to be able to go home, it was now the 4th of July. It had been a long time to be away from home. I cleaned out all my drawers; I had acquired so much stuff, cards, letters, pictures etc. My sister Tracey was fully aware as like everyone else that I had missed out on the first part of her life, when people have babies they take pictures, lots of pictures, with being so ill, it's something that didn't seem important, but it was it was very important. These pictures would be what I missed out on, precious moments in time with my daughter. Un aware to me, Tracey was taking pictures left right and centre, I think I had my very own flipper book of Ellie's life until then, and they say am snap happy! These photographs that she had taken were very precious to me, and I am so grateful, and always will be to Tracey for taking them for me.

I had lots of things to take away with me, things people had bought, and I could have opened a shop for the amount of teddies me and Ellie had been given. I decided I wasn't going to take them all home, and asked on of the nurses to send a few to the baby and children's wards. My stuff packed, and walls bare, Ellie asleep in her cot, this was it, my road to being me again, and being able to look after Ellie. I had lots of medication to take away, and was still on lots of different types of drugs, I would have to take some in the morning and some at night, and they stressed how important to my recovery it was for me to take them, and had words with My Mum and Dad and Mark to remind me.

I rang everyone I knew to tell them that I was coming home; they all seemed as excited as me. Some of the student nurses were talking and listening to music, they smiled when they saw me and asked me if I was okay, and that they had heard I was to be 'released tomorrow' I walked around the ward looking at all the beds and talking to people, looking around and seeing how broken some people were due to unfortunate events in their life. It saddened me and as much as I wanted to get out of this place, I wished there was more I could do to help the ones I was leaving behind.

The morning came so quickly, and before I knew it I was bathing Ellie, and changing her ready to take her home, I loved saying this 'home'. Mum and Dad had rang as I wanted Mark to pick me up and bring me home, like we planned when Ellie was born but this time I was home to stay. Mum and Dad said they would be along the day after to let me settle in to see how I was doing. Mum and Dad had lived in Liverpool, and whilst I was ill, had moved back to Ellesmere Port to help me get better, so they were only down the road now.

Mark arrived, in his faded jeans and cap, no change there then, he always wore his cap, and it was nice that something looked the same. I flung my arms around him, and after a chat with the nurse manager, we were walking out the door. I will never forget what the nurse Manager had said to me that day. "As lovely as it was to have met you Grace" she said smiling, "I hope that we will never see you again" and she gave me a hug. I immediately knew what she meant, because for me to go back would mean I was ill.

They waved me off as we left, and Claire the nurse had a tear in her eye as she said goodbye to me and Ellie. We were walking out of the building, Mark holding on to Ellie, and me holding the bags and bottles, the Sun was cracking the flags outside, and I couldn't wait to get my Jumper off. We were quiet on the way home. I just soaked in the sunshine, and thought about what I wanted to do when I got home. A hot bath and pancakes that's what I wanted I decided.

Instead of pulling up at our house, we pulled up at Marks mum and dad's house. "Why are we here" I said "'we are going to stay here tonight" Again this should have all been prepared and discussed before I even came home. "I want to go home", was all I could say.' Please grace Mums making a home coming tea," "and we will stay here tonight and go home tomorrow". 'Ok' was all I could say but if it meant we could go home tomorrow, it was only one day.

We went inside, the house was buzzing, there were loads of Marks family asking me how I was, and picking Ellie up, and kissing her, I got asked how I was feeling so many times, I sounded like a parrot. I suddenly felt very tired and wanted to lie down and have some time to myself. In the hospital I hated the alone time. But gradually I became used to it, and even wanted it at times. I missed it.

I needed to sit and reflect, and to be still and I needed quiet. Ellie was fine and I went upstairs on Marks bed. After about 15 minutes Dave Marks dad came up, and brought me a cup of tea. "Are you okay babe"? He said. "Yeah I'm alright"; "it all feels strange". He said that everybody had left, and it was just us, and Carol was making a roast just for me. He brushed the hair out of my face and said "this is just the beginning Woody" "you can start all over again, just you Mark and Ellie". I smiled, I must have fallen asleep, as when I woke up, I had been covered up, and Mark was sitting by me on the bed. 'Hello stranger' he said. I flung my arms around him, and I told him how much I had missed him, and that it was all going to be okay. 'Let's just take one day at a time' he said and we went down for tea.

The next day we were going home, to our house, I wanted to get there as soon as possible, and be surrounded by my things. I turned the key in the lock, when I walked in, the curtains were drawn, and it was dark and stank, musty and sweaty. I opened them, everywhere was covered in dust, and the place was a mess. There were dishes that had been there so long, they had gone green with mould. There were crisps packets and chocolate wrappers on the floor, like what I and Mark used to do when we watched a film, except we hadn't. There were bits of plate and cup, broken on the floor, from when I had first gotten ill, the place didn't look like home. It looked horrible. I sat down on the couch, and I suddenly didn't have the energy to do a thing. I wanted to cry. "Mark said 'I have been busy with work and stuff, and i have been at Mum and Dads mostly since you've been in hospital', but ill sort it"

There was a knock on the door. It was My Mum, "'Hello are we all settled in" she said. As she walked in the room she stopped mid sentence and looked at the house. Mark said he was going to get milk and some food and he took Ellie with him. As soon as he was gone, she started up. "What the bloody hell has he brought you back to!" she screamed. She could see the bits of crockery that I had smashed when it had all started, and she began picking them up. She was livid. When I told her that I had only been there ten minutes she was going berserk. "He should have had this bloody house ready for you when you came home with Ellie'!! And you should have stayed here last night not there you should have been at home". I started to cry, I didn't want to be in hospital and I didn't want to be here, I didn't know where I wanted to be, I felt more lost than I thought I could. My mum with tears in her eyes said 'come on' giving me a cuddle as she did, "we will have this place spick and span in no time". She rang my sister's house, and asked them if they could come over.

My sister Beryl and my sister Sue came. Between the three of them, they filled three bin bags with rubbish, and cleaned the entire house, and hoovered the lot. It looked lovely, and smelt of peach and jasmine air freshener, not a broken plate or cup in sight. It looked like my house, my house that I had a long time ago, and my house that I loved to clean. As much as I wanted things done, not just for the house, things done for me things done for Ellie, my mind couldn't seem to cope with the effort of it all, and as crazy as it sounds, I forgot how to do things, normal things like, making a cup of tea, it seemed too much, and my hands would shake at times. I just couldn't do it; I would avoid it like it was out to get me or something. It was odd and I didn't understand it. I wanted things done but I just didn't have the energy or will to do them.

My Mum and sisters were just finishing off, when Mark came in with Ellie, he had been hours. "Where have you been" I said. "I have been shopping and took Ellie for a walk in the pram". "Wow the house looks great," he said; "I was going to do it" he said. '

"Mm yeah were you" my mum said" "well it's done now" "Just look after Grace and your daughter now", "coz we've done it" she said. A little too harshly, I thought. She made a drink, and then said to the girls that they should go. They kissed us all and left. Mark helped me bath Ellie and change her. In the hospital, I had had staff there on tap to help me, and in the last two weeks of me being there, I didn't ask for their help, and I did it myself, but they were there. Somehow coming home, seemed to knock my confidence with Ellie, I felt like I couldn't do it. "You can grace" "you have too" "am back at work on Monday". I felt like I had been kicked in the stomach when he said this. "But I have only been home a day" I sobbed. Today was Saturday, that meant after Sunday I would be on my own in the house with Ellie. The thought of it terrified me. My Mum came and also so did the CPN Dawn, she was lovely, and caring and put me at ease straight away. "Its going to feel strange, for a while, but you will be fine grace" "you have lots of love and support to help you".

The morning came and he left for work. "Ill come back at dinner" he said. Dinner time came and went he never came. I hardly saw him, and when I did it was strained, and he would tell me I was holding Ellie wrong, or get cross with me, if I didn't go to her straight away when she was crying. I was a nervous wreck.

Weeks passed and it was soon August, and it was one of the hottest summers we had ever had. I rang my Mum all the time and she would come round, and take Ellie for a walk with me outside, something I had never done before, something that you take for granted. I was like a broken shell, I wasn't running around angry or saying mad things like I did when I was in hospital, but I wasn't grace, I was empty, and had no confidence in myself what so ever. It was like there was no person behind my eyes. Mark became very distant, I had only been home a few weeks, and he was spending more time away from me, from home and from Ellie. He was on call most of the time, and then one day he came home got changed in to his best clothes, and aftershave and said he would see me later.' where are you going"I said. "Out" "ill be back later", and with that he shut the door and left. I wanted to cry, I was desperate too, but I couldn't, I curled myself in a ball on the settee and went to sleep.

Because I was seeing so little of Mark, I occupied myself with Ellie and trying to be her mum. She had a beautiful smile, she was so good, and I would put her in the bath with me and play with her, I got into quite a good routine with her, I washed her by myself, changed her, and she was in bed asleep for 7pm and would sleep all the way through till 7am the next morning, I felt like I was doing it right, well some of it anyway. Then she began to get teeth. She would scream and get ill, every time she cut one, and her little cheeks would enflame, I would be up till all hours every night, I had never been so tired in my life. I came down to make myself a coffee, and ended up pouring coffee in to Ellies milk bottle.

I asked Mark for help, but he was never there, always on call, and when he was, he needed to go to sleep. I got through it, I would ring Mum and cry at the bottom of the stairs, saying "I can't do this mum" "it's too hard" to a reply of' "yes you can Grace" "you are a survivor and this is a part of being a mum", "I know your tired but you will get through it you can do this love you can". The reassurance helped, and Mum gave me the confidence to keep trying, and to give me that little push. Carol Marks mum would come and visit me on her way home from work, with new clothes for Ellie, and a box of chocolates for me, she offered to have Ellie a lot at weekends, and when the teething was bad, I needed a break, but the health visitor said her bond with me was more important than anything else right now, and she should stay with me, so I did what they had said. Even though I was tired and felt like I needed a break, I wanted her with me and I needed her with me. When it started to ease I let Carol take her sometimes for me, and she took her home for tea, and gave her a bath so she was all ready for me to go to bed. The minute she left I fell asleep straight away, and she woke me up on her return, I was knackered. I had people helping in shifts, sounds funny but people were there but let me have my peace. Pam was over the road and helped a lot. She made lovely tea's for me, and arranged Mum and Baby groups for me. I never had anything like that, because I was ill, that took over everything else. She even came with me to one, and it wasn't as bad as I thought. It was babies playing together and looking at the baby toys etc. And the mums would sit and have a chat.

On the day that I went there was hardly anyone there and this pleased me so much. I couldn't face a load of strangers. There were young mums like me and the two I met on my visit, were quite shy and polite and we spoke about how bad it was with the teething and the tiredness. Just that one small conversation with a stranger made all the difference to me, I felt like a 'normal' person for half an hour, a 'normal' mum. I thanked Pam so much, I didn't go all the time, but it was nice to know that it was there if I needed it.

Mum would come every other day and ring me everyday. Dad popped in to say hello and never stayed long. The CPN's visits would be 3 times a week to begin with and then went down to two and then once a week gradually. I had a visit from the midwife once a fortnight also. My sisters would visit too. But everyone thought that Mark was there so didn't worry as much, but he wasn't he was always at work or out.

I found being in the house alone hard at times, but welcomed it when I had lots of visitors. It was strange. I didn't want lots of people coming in to my house, but I didn't want the emptiness either. I tried hard to keep the house well kept, but it seemed to take longer than it did before. If things broke like a glass or a bulb I would get very upset, as if it was the end of the world, and I would have to remind myself that it wasn't. I became very sensitive and at times paranoid. My mum could comment on something in a good way, and I would twist it and make it into an insult or criticism. She was so patient. I had lots of time with Ellie and when she wasn't crying with her teeth, I loved it and I loved her company. But when I couldn't comfort her or make her better when she was crying, I would become angry and frustrated with myself, and would almost want to be a mummy another time. Sounds mad I was a mummy but at times I didn't want the responsibility of it all, at times it got too much. I tried my best to have a routine at home like I did at hospital. Ellie had a bedtime a bath time times for her meals, I even had a time that I sat in the garden with her. I cleaned the house and wheeled her round in her pram and spoke to her while I did it.

The days flew by.

Chapter 16

I AM LEAVING YOU

Before I knew it, I was keeping the house straight and tidy, and doing everything for Ellie. I was like a robot, but I was doing it. I had been home a while now, it was the mid August and hot. All the windows in the street were open, as were the doors and all the kids in the street would play out, it was a nice street, the neighbours were friendly, and everybody looked out for one another.

Pam would often come over check I was okay, and bring me a gorgeous tea to eat, she was a fabulous cook, so I never refused, soon the baby weight I managed to keep off had started to creep back up, I was eating and looking better, and everybody seemed happy about this.

I was missing Mark, desperately, he was always at work, or there was always somewhere he had to go. When he did make it back but the problem I was struggling with at present was going outside. I don't know how it started but I would feel like it was closing in on me when I was outside, I wouldn't be able to catch my breath, and if I didn't know someone really well, I couldn't talk to them, and have a normal conversation with them. I would go outside, and feel like I could not breathe. Without realising it, I was suffering from panic attacks. Because I did not understand what it was, I did not tell anybody at first. It would happen when I ate, but mostly when I left the house. I went from not being able to cry, to not being able to stop crying.

I felt like I was a complete mess, but everyone kept telling me how well I was doing.

Mark was expected home one day at 7pm. I decided that I was going to make myself look nice, and I found some of my old make up to wear, and the bra and knickers that my sister Sue brought on a visit. They had not been worn yet, perfect opportunity I thought, id had a shower washed my hair and Pam had lent me some perfume, as id had none. I looked at myself in my cracked mirror in my bedroom. I looked all right, I thought, and began getting Ellie ready for bed.

I was just drying her on my knee, and had her bedclothes ready when Mark burst through the door. "Guess what," I said before he had chance to say anything. "I've made tea for you and me". Not a major achievement I know, but at that time, it was huge for me to be able to do something like that. Our diet consisted of pot noodles and beans on toast, and when we did eat well, it was because Pam had cooked for his Mum, my Mum, or us.

I had made a lovely curry and rice, home cooked with chicken just like my mum used to make. I spent half of the day on the phone, going through the method with mum to get it just right. "I am not hungry Grace' he said, his face looked pale. "What is wrong" I said trying to stop Ellie wriggling off my knee as I dried her body. He began to cry, I wrapped Ellie up, and ran to where he was, and said; "whatever it is we can sort it what's the matter"? "I don't love you anymore" "I am leaving you," he said.

The words hung in the air; I almost did not believe him. I sat down with Ellie, and finished putting her bedclothes on. I did not speak. "Did you hear me Grace"? I put Ellie in her bouncer chair. "Yes I heard you," I said calmly. "I know im not like I used to be but I will get better", "just give me time please Mark". "Grace I have felt like this for a long time". "Is there someone else?" I asked. "No" he said firmly. He began packing his bag, and sorting things that he needed around the house. I was in a daze; I concentrated all my thoughts on Ellie and getting her to bed. When she was asleep, I helped him ball socks up, and pack underwear, as we were going on holiday or something almost trying to block out what was happening.

He kissed Ellie on the head asleep in her cot, and he turned and said, "I will come see you and Ellie in a few days". He closed the door behind him. I sat on the couch, and cried and cried. I rang His Mum frantically, telling them what had happened. His dad answered the phone, and said "what"? "He's said what"? "Does not worry Grace" "we will sort this out okay" it will all be okay"?

I went to bed that night, and thought about what had just happened I felt more alone than ever before.

The next morning, I tried to ring him, but his voicemail was on, and he never answered. I went in the bathroom, and straight away had spotted his tooth brush was not there, more tears, I cried so much the following day I was making Ellie cry, and I knew I had to stop, I was exhausting myself. I tried to carry on as normal but I felt like I had my heart removed, I had panic attack after panic attack. Everyone began to hear of the news, was all shocked, and did not know what to say to me. One person that did know what to say was my mum, "That Bastard" you have only been home a few weeks"! "Don't worry love we are all here for you'". The more she slagged him off the more I defended him. It did not seem as big a shock to everyone else as it was to me.

He rang me two days later, asked after Ellie, and asked how I was. I sobbed down the phone, "please don't go' 'I love you", "I need you right now"' "I need you more than ever" "I miss you". I was crying so hard he could not understand what I was saying. He said he had to go, and that he would come and see me the following day. The next day I waited and waited like an anxious puppy waiting for him to turn up. He did with his dad; he kissed Ellie and gave me a hug. "Are you alright?" he said. I was thrilled to see him Dave looked sad, and squeezed me tight, and asked how Ellie was and tickled her. H e kept avoiding my eyes. "I hope you don't mind but I want to take my telly". He had bought a huge widescreen TV and stand while I was in hospital and my little portable was now in the bedroom. "Err yeah; okay you bought it where's it going"? I asked frantically. "I will be living at my Mum and Dads for a while till I sort somewhere to live". It was official he was not coming back, I sobbed at the door, and Dave sat in his car, he could not face me.

Mark kissed me said how sorry he was and when he got chance would give me some money. I did not care about money, all I cared about was him and me and Ellie our family. We had never even begun to be one. I was distraught. He would buy Ellie clothes and toys, and even a designer three-wheeler pram, and instead of coming himself, he would send them with his Mum and Dad when they came to visit. The visits got less and less. I would have no shame or dignity, I would ring him all the time, telling him how much I loved and missed him, he was always busy and always had to go. I was completely heartbroken. I was still sick, and now mending a broken heart. I cried all the time. My eyes stood out on stalks, and the weight dropped off me, I was now under nine stone, something I had not been since I was in school. My clothes hung off me, and I looked and felt a mess.

I would spend all my time crying in my room, or on the phone to my mum, it was unbearable. Then a letter arrived from the mortgage company. Dear Miss Wood, as we have had no reply from you about any of the arrears, if you do not contact us within 14 days we will be evicting you from your property... I could not believe it, as well as losing my mind, my daughter for a while, and my partner, it looked like I was about to lose my house. I rang Mark straight away, and to my surprise, he answered. 'Hello' I explained what the letter had said, because the house was in my name, he could not sort any of it out he said. "I told them you were in hospital". "But you have been paying it haven't you"? He said that he had contacted the social security office and that only the interest was being paid, and because I was in hospital, and did not need the benefits I was on that had been used to pay for it.

He said he had to get back to work, and the line went dead. My body started to shake I could not believe it. I rang them and then rang the relevant people; I was on the phone for hours trying to sort the mess out. It had turned out that it was arranged that just the interest on the mortgage be to be paid until I was fit and well and that it would not be a problem, and part of my benefit was to cover it. Wires had been crossed somewhere down the line and none of it had been paid for months. I quickly sorted out the situation, and decided I should pay as much as I could to pay it off and get out of the red. When I had managed to pay this, and what I owed plus my bills I was left with £39 pounds per week to live on. Not a lot, but Ellie was getting milk vouchers and I could even buy baby food with them too. So that was not too bad, I hardly ate and when I did, it consisted of toast. The money seemed to run through my fingers. With buying nappies, and her growing so quickly, I was constantly buying shoes, and clothes.

I rang Mark and he agreed he would give me £200 per month. This would help me so much. I was still completely heartbroken over Mark, and whenever I thought for a moment about everything, or wherever I was, the tears would flow. Nobody knew what to do, or what to say to me, so in the end they said nothing at all. It was the worst time of my life. I would look at Ellie when she slept, and I would realise the responsibility of being a parent, and now the responsibility seemed to be all on my head. The thought terrified me. I would look at her, while she was asleep, or in the bath, or on my knee, and I would think to myself "my god what have I done". I would ring my mum all the time, sometimes in the middle of the night, she would never be cross, and she would make a coffee, sit up, and talk to me for hours. Telling me how it was going to be okay and it will just click in to place and I would stop feeling this way about Ellie. "But what if it doesn't mum" I would say. She would get upset and say. "Do you remember when you were ill, and you used to say to me, "mum will I ever get better"? "Will I ever get out of here"? "Well look at you now", "at home looking after your baby and out of hospital". "This is just your post natal depression Grace you will get better I promise you, and when you do this will all seem like a bad dream".

However negative I was, she was always there, pulling me up, making me strong. I did not realise at the time that no sooner she got off the phone to me. She would be crying and worrying herself to sleep about me.

The negative feelings I had towards being a parent, and the pain of realising Mark wasn't coming back, was too much to bear, when I wasn't crying I was quiet, I hardly spoke, and hardly ate, I felt lost and alone, and trapped. Amongst all of the feelings that I had, there was a beautiful little baby wanting me to be her Mummy and love her. I constantly asked Mum to come round, and when she was not helping me and doing things for Ellie to give me a break, Carol Mark's mum was there more than happy to take over. Between the two of them, it was easy to pass on the responsibility of caring for Ellie on to them. I wanted to know she was okay, and that she was safe and warm, but I could not hug her, smell her, and play with her properly, it was like something was missing. I looked at mothers and you could see they had something that I did not have? I felt like I was looking after her, but I was not her mummy.

Sometimes I would pick her up out of the cot, and say 'come on El let aunty Grace change your nappy'. I would hear myself say it, and I would think she is my daughter I am not her aunty.

My Mum soon clicked on that, I was running away from the responsibility of being a mum; she knew I was terrified of doing it wrong, and the hopelessness that I felt. However, she also knew that too many people were interfering and that I needed to be kept an eye on, but to be left to get on with things.

My sisters were worried about me, and would often say to my mum "what if something happens"? "What if she has a relapse"? "What if she leaves Ellie"? Mum said; "she has been through so much", and I know she's trying to get better and heal over Mark", "but the most important thing right now is Grace and Ellie". "She needs to know we are there but Ellie needs her Mummy and with looking after her on her own, that little girl will see her through". I had support off the CPN, the health visitor, and the midwife they would pop in, say hello, and ask after me and how I was. I had all these people to talk too, and be helped by, but I did not want to talk or to be helped I wanted Mark back and my life.

The phone calls from Mum were always there, as with everyone else's. However, the visits were less frequent. In addition, when I asked for help with Ellie or if somebody would take her. Mum would find an excuse not to come as often. I remember saying '

"But I need a bath mum"? My reply was brief. "I had 8 kids and I could have a bath". "Take Ellie with you, or sit her in her little chair and let her watch you have a bath". To me it felt like Mum just didn't want to have Ellie or help me, but what she was really doing was forcing me to do what was needed to be done by me, and me alone. I did not realise that by doing this, I would gradually fall in love with my baby, and catch up on all the things I had missed or could not remember. The pain I was feeling would ease over time; I would forget how much things cost, and how much she depended on me, and the responsibility of it all. I would realise that I was not useless or hopeless, I was like any other new mum just inexperienced, and with time, and I would hopefully figure out what I was doing and love her unconditionally like any other mum does.

This took some time, when I was not completely shattered or crying, Ellie would need feeding, winding, changing, clothes needed washing, and ironing, that is without anything I needed for myself. The lists of things to be done were endless. However, I did it. I would get up everyday and do it. One night she was crying, really crying with real tears rolling down her face, she had had a temperature, her little cheeks were red and swollen with teething, and she had not slept right for a few days. I woke up in the middle of the night and tried everything, I gave her calpol, changed her fed her you name it I did it, she did not want to know. I rang my Mum in floods of tears sitting on the floor. "I can't do this mum im a useless mother" "I quit". My Mum laughed down the line. "Why are you laughing?" I demanded to know. "She's your baby and she needs you," "and you need her", "when you're a mum quit just isn't a word in the vocabulary". I sobbed down the phone, "mum I can't do this" "I can't' it's too hard" "and she doesn't like me". "Of course she likes you"; "she loves you, "you're her mummy" "you are just finding your feet" "it will be okay".

Mum went through with me all of the things I had tried to get her to stop crying. I ticked them off mentally that I had done them as she was going along. "I've done all of those things and she's still crying".

"I know one thing you haven't done"' "what"? I said. "Have you cuddled her and held her close", "and sang to her"? It was one thing I had not done; in fact, it was one thing I steered clear of. I did everything for her, she was washed dressed, ate well drank well, when she was poorly or teethed I gave her all the right things and did all of the things I was supposed to, but I never gave her or showed her any love.

When Mum got off the phone, it was gone 1am. She was still sobbing. I picked her up out of the cot and grabbed her dummy; I sat on the old rocking chair, in her room. We had bought it Mark and me, when I was pregnant when we did up her room. It was second hand and had a few scratches on it, but it was comfortable and it rocked. I had never sat on it. I picked up her soft blanket, wrapped it around her, gave her the dummy to suck and cuddled her in. I wrapped my arms around her, and rocked backwards and forwards, and stroked her little hair, her fingers were entwined with mine. She stopped crying, and just stared at me.

I looked at her for the first time, and felt so guilty; none of this was her fault. She was beautiful, tiny and perfect in every single way she was my baby. I sat and cried as she fell asleep on my lap, I wasn't crying for Mark, or because I was scared, I was crying because I realised as much as Ellie needed me, I needed her I loved her. This feeling this 'rush of love' people talk about when their baby is born, I did not get it. Sitting in the dark, on a warm summer night, rocking and humming 'Amazing Grace' to Ellie, I finally got it.

THE HOLE IN MY CHEST...

The tears that fell could fill an Ocean,
The hole in my chest, the despair, the emotion.

I ached, I cried, I longed for you,
The pain I felt was raw and true.

I needed you; I would scream your name…? But an answer never came.
What's happening? So confused? So sad… you left.
You ripped out my heart and left this gape in my chest.

It was like a part of me had died,
Right along with my soul, and my heart and my pride.

Every time I saw your face,
My heart would thump, and then break.

Stood in the street, with my heart in the road,
You moved on, me and Ellie we were out in the cold.

I grew up, I grew strong, and I mended me,
I realised that we were never meant to be.

Grace Sharrock

Chapter 17

CHERYL

I started to bond with Ellie, more than I thought I possibly could. I cuddled her more, kissed her more, and the crying that seemed endless at first seemed to vanish. I was thinking about what I was going through, and the pain I felt, and the mess I was in. I needed to stop, and think about Ellie and what she needed, and what she needed was a Mummy. I wanted Mark back so desperately, but my main priority now and from this day, would always be Ellie.

I started to combat my fear of going outside, I wouldn't force myself, and If I saw anybody, I would panic, and the sweat would drench around my neck, and I would run home with Ellie and get the pram in the door as fast as I could. I built it up gradually, it wasn't easy at first, and I would take a brown paper bag out with me, in case I couldn't catch my breath, and hyperventilated, like my doctor had told me. I would get to the end of the road, then I would go a bit further and end up at the corner shop, and before I knew it, I was visiting my Mum, a half a mile away.

My mum would say how proud she was of me making it this far. "Maybe you could go to town or the park soon". The thought of loads of people terrified me; I took it one day at a time. Ellie looked so much better for the fresh air, and on a warm sunny day, I was glad of it too. We sat at a park bench and I realised Ellie had never tasted ice cream. I decided that when the ice cream van came the next day, I was going to buy her a Mr. whippy ice cream, with strawberry sauce. The next day when I heard the familiar sound of the ice cream van coming down the road, I did just that. She sat with a towel on the couch with me, and she looked at it curiously as if it were an alien, I held it for her and brought it to her mouth, it felt so good to be doing a first with Ellie, something she hadn't done before just me and her, and I was excited by the thought of it, and liked to think of me in years to come telling her what she was like when she had her first ice cream. She looked at it and then opened her slobbery lips and took some into her mouth. The face she pulled was so funny! It was cold and she did not like it one bit! She did not like it, but she kept on going back for more! Her face was a picture.

I took my camera out of my bag, and took one of her holding her first ice cream. She would hold out her arms and say 'urgh' urgh' for me to pick her up, it felt nice that she wanted me, and she began to make noises with her mouth, a word she started to use was 'hiya' we would be out in the pram and she would see a dog, a lamppost and say 'hiya' to it. She made me laugh all the time, and I enjoyed being with her. But when Carol had her or my mum, I would miss her desperately, which was good and natural. However, I would ring all the time, and check for silly things, making sure she was okay. 'Has she got enough nappies'? She likes her food slightly heated to take the chill off' have I packed calpol'?

I knew I had done all of these things, it was an excuse to see that she was okay, and an excuse to make sure. I do not know why but I did not want them to know I was missing her. Her staying away and me having a break, didn't happen as much, and pretty soon when Carol would ask if she could take her like she had done before, and I said 'no' it was like a shock to her system, and she seemed pretty put out by it. I wasn't being funny, but the way I felt about her, and how I had started to feel things like normal mums did, and how I missed her so much when she was gone, I wanted to hold onto that and make up for all the time that she was away from me. And it was not because I thought that it should be like that, or someone had told me, it was different now, I really did want to be with her, and I wanted her home with me.

Mark would come, and knock on the door, I would make out his shadow in the glass, and my heart would thump, every time I saw him I reverted to being 16 again. He would still kiss me, and hug me, and when I asked him to stay he would not and he would pull away. Every time it happened, I would feel crushed, but I would keep it in, as I was glad, he wanted to see Ellie. He got a shock when he saw her and said how big she was and how well she looked. He said he had not seen much of her, when his mum and dad had Ellie for a visit, as he had been out, or on call. He would be working away with his job a lot now he said but he would call when he could.

The times he came became very few and after a while, he stopped coming at all. I realised ringing him all the time was not helping, and as much as it was killing me, I decided that all my energy needed to be focused on Ellie. Before I knew it, it was October. My Mum had said that she had seen Maria, I really wanted to see her and to talk to her, but I was told some of the things that I had said to her when I was ill. I felt like I could not face her. My mum said that that is exactly how Maria was feeling, and that I should pluck up the courage to ring her. I put it off for a few days, and thought of all the little scenarios of what could be said on the phone. What if she thought I was a mad freak and had found a new best friend? The thought of it nearly choked me. I could really do with a friend right now, and she had always been at the back of my mind, I missed her, and how she was, her making me laugh.

Up until this point in my life, she had always been there. I

Was having the worst time of it, and wanted to share it all with her, and for her to tell me what she thought. Not just because I needed her at that time, but because I missed her, I missed her perfume on my clothes, when she would call for a cuppa, I missed her moaning at my CD'S I missed her telling me to stop bloody cleaning up and talk to her while she was having a fag out me bedroom window. I just missed my friend, but had no idea how to get her back.

'Why don't you just bloody phone her' my mum said one day, and I decided that is exactly what I was going to do. I picked the phone up, and dialled her familiar number, it was mad I hadn't spoken to her for over 6 months, there was weeks and months I could not remember, but I could remember her phone number as if it were my own. I heard a voice and quickly put it down. My heart was beating faster, and I panicked what do I say? 'Hiya ye know yer best mate Grace that you used to know? Ye know the one who smashed your back garden up and threatened to kill ye? Well i am better now can we be best mates again?' I had no idea where I was going to start, should I apologise. I didn't even remember half of the things I had said and did, and I was ill, but what do I say? I did not have a clue. I wished that I were not on medication just so I could have a few glasses of chardonnay for Dutch courage.

I rang again, and this time she answered. 'hello' she said, my voice was dry and my mouth went numb.' hello' she said again.

In fear of her thinking she had got a dirty phone call or even put it down, I said 'hello' back. Without me even saying anything she said 'hi Grace' 'how are you?' She sounded just like she always did, and without her knowing, the tears were tripping my face as she spoke. 'I am fine I said' I lied, I was a nervous wreck.

' I was wondering if you would like to come round and see Ellie and see me, I would love to talk to you' I said shakily. She said that it was lovely to hear from me and that she would love to come and see me soon but she was busy that day, and how about at the weekend when she was not working. I agreed and we arranged for the coming weekend. It was a short conversation, like before, but with more warmth from me, I think. She sounded so great, I wanted to climb down the phone and hug her. I wiped my tears and rang my mum.' That is great news she said.

The following weekend seemed to drag, and in a way, I was glad. I was having conversations with her and myself in my head and wondered how it would pan out. I was desperately hoping for the best, and did not expect it straight away; I just wanted the chance to explain, and the chance of my very valued friendship back. I loved her to pieces (and still do), she had never had a sister she was one of five, and had four brothers, when we were growing up her mum said she felt she had six kids as I was there so much. Maria always said I was like the sister she had never had.

Before I knew it, she was knocking on the door. Ellie was asleep in her pram, and the house was clean and tidy, all for the smell of burnt toast.

I walked to the door, she had never knocked on my door before, and she had a key and would always walk in or let herself in and shout' only me get the kettle on'. I opened the door, it was teaming with rain, and she stood at the door with a plant in her hands. 'Hi' she said 'hi' I said in quite a high-pitched voice, and we just stood looking at one another, while she was getting soaked. 'Ye going to let me in' she said with a smile and a half laugh. 'Oh sorry yeah come in'. The plant looked like it had been drowned, and mud was dripping on to the wooden floor. 'Oh sorry she said' and tried to wipe it with her fingers. She seemed as nervous as I did. I wiped it up and said do you want a coffee. I would love one she said. As we walked in to the living room, she saw Ellie asleep in her pram. She had only seen her when she was a baby when she was first born, and once when I first went in the hospital when Mark had brought her round. 'Oh grace she has grown so much she is beautiful' she said. I beamed with pride, 'I know she isn't she I said' covering her up.

We sat with our coffees on our knees, and she went to say something at the same time as me after quite a long pause. 'No sorry you go first' no you go first'. We were being very polite with one another. Then all of a sudden very quickly I said' i am so sorry for what I said and what I did' She looked at me, and said your mum told me what happened and why you did what you did. I told her what it was like, and how when I remembered things it was as if I was looking at someone else remembering. She recalled to me what I had said to her that day, and she had tears in her eyes, I wanted to run over to her and kiss her cheeks and tell her how much I missed and loved her. Instead, I stayed sitting.

We talked about Mark leaving and she seemed to want to change the subject, but she was shocked and sorry. The coffee was cold, and she made an excuse to leave. She got to the door, and when she did, I turned and said how much I had missed her, and that I loved her, the tears were rolling down my cheeks, and when I looked up her face was wet too. She grabbed me and hugged me so tight, I hugged her twice as hard, and I did not want to let go. 'That was a GBH hug an a half' I said, and she laughed, it was so lovely to see her laugh and smile it was infectious and made me smile too. We did not need to make 'arrangements' anymore, it wasn't cold and awkward, we just went back to being Grace and Maria again, just like we had always had. She was lovely with me, I did not have to explain myself, or apologise, and she would not accept it anyway. 'You were ill and did not know what you were saying, so why should you apologise' she said.

I had my mum to thank for talking to Maria and keeping in touch, and explaining my illness, so she should understand. I had so much to thank my mum for. When I went to get my benefits and got my money from the post office that day, I went to the market and bought my mum a huge bouquet of flowers, and wrote on the card' love ye mum thanks for everything'. She rang me the morning she got them and cried down the phone, 'that's what mums are for' one day Ellie will be buying you flowers, thank you sweetheart she said. While I was ill, I felt like, I had lost everything, bit-by-bit things were slipping away from me, and Getting Maria back gave me hope that my life would get back on track. I would cry for Mark lots, I would ring her in floods of tears, and she would never be busy or be sick of hearing me cry, sometimes she would cry along with me. Hugging me and making endless cups of tea, sometimes she would come straight from work and stay till really late, whenever I needed her she was there, for Ellie and for me, it was like all those months of not being in each others lives hadn't happened, she was like a rock for me, and she helped me to keep going, even when I felt like I couldn't. She really was and still is the best friend I could ever have wished for. Ellie adored her, and she would come in the room, and she would be all smiles for her, she was always buying her clothes and toys and spoiling her.

The tears were endless, the nights were the worst, and I felt so lonely, I sat up one night going through photographs, I am what's known in my family as snap happy! And Carol and Dave would always tease me and say 'put that bloody camera away' I had tons of pictures, pictures and letters I had sent Mark over the years, and photos from school and me and him standing by a Christmas tree in his Mum and Dad's when I was 18, I had the worst haircut in the world, I was so skinny and my hair looked like a birds nest, he was covered in spots with his hair at the front flicked up with gel, we both looked like Cheshire cats grinning, with my arms wrapped around him.

I remember falling in love with him, and how much I loved him when the picture was taken and how much I still felt the same. I was convinced my illness had sent him away and he could not look at me like he did before, he saw me at my worst and he must have looked at me like a freak. I felt embarrassed and desperately wanted to talk to him and hold him and for him to tell me it was all going to be okay. The tears would roll, and I could spend an hour trying to figure out what went wrong. I put all the photos away, no I am not doing this I am going to be strong.

I put the photos away, I was going to get him back somehow, and my family our family was going to have a chance. My aunty Deanie who lived in Norfolk, (she was not really my aunty but we all called her that, she was my mums best friend) had called my mum, she asked if I would like to go and stay with her for a week for a break. I think really she was trying to give my mum a break from all the worry, and let someone else take over for a while. Ellie was 8 months old, she had heard all about her, but had never seen her. We took the train, Ellie and me, she looked at all the trees whizzing past in the window, and she was so good and slept for most of the way. When I arrived she was there with her partner Wally, waiting for me at the station. It had been years since I had seen her, but I recognised her straight away. She hugged me so tight and squeezed Ellie too. When we got to her house, she had thought of everything, she had even borrowed a cot, and blankets. She had nappies, wipes food milk, you name it, and it was there. She had asked my mum what was needed and she bought it all while I was on the train. She instantly made me feel at home, but I did not know how to behave, or what I was supposed to do with myself.

I did not sleep the first night, and looked out of my huge bedroom window, Norfolk was beautiful, loads of trees and canal boats it was lovely, and the air was fresh and clean, and it was nice to get away and have company. We would walk around the market stalls, which I liked, and go for walks. Her partner Wally was a manager at the local chocolate factory, he took me for a tour, it was fantastic, and it smelled gorgeous. He took me to see how all the chocolate was made and how it ended up in the boxes. He let me try some and he filled a bin bag with every type they made for me. The thing I liked about being at Aunty Deanie's was the quiet. They were simple people that liked simple pleasures, they did not watch much TV, they liked the radio, and they did crosswords and drank wine. I was till ill from my post natal depression, and I still felt like I was on a roller coaster at times, and I wanted to get off, to get away from myself and my head and own thoughts. Here was the perfect place to do just that. I could sit, think, and just be quiet without anyone asking me if I was okay or if I wanted a cup of tea.

I was sick of bloody tea, for 8 months I had had every type of tea you could ever have, weak, strong, cold, Luke warm, chamomile, fruit you name it I was offered it. My family and friends (and I do even to this day) offer tea in times of crisis every time I had been in tears or had just punched a doctor in the hospital (as you do) I was told to keep calm and have a nice cup of tea PISS OFF WITH THE TEA!!! I wanted to shout but I never did. Here was never offered it, I could just help myself, and it was a refreshing change. It was calm, and I relaxed next to her beautiful roaring fire, with Ellie asleep on my knee. I would ring mum at night and she said I sounded good, and I felt like I felt better, just for the change. I text Mark lots telling him what I was up to, and how Ellie was, but he never text back. He must be busy I told myself ill try him again tomorrow.

Wally went out with friends one night, so it was just me Deanie and Ellie, she said how about a girl's night just us, and I liked the sound of that. I got Ellie in bed, sat with her waiting for a programme with Julie Walters to come on, Aunty Deanie loved her, and she was playing a scouser, who lived on a rough council estate. It reminded her of her and Mum when they were young, she told me stories of Mum and what she was like when she was young, her beehive hair and crooked teeth, she made mum sound like a bit of a rebel, and it was lovely to hear of her being young and carefree. We chatted and watched the programme. She drank Red wine, and offered me a glass; I had not had a drink for months because I was on my medication. I thought what the hell and accepted a glass. Before I knew it I had had four glasses of strong red wine, I was as they say as pissed as a fart. The lovely tea I had eaten with auntie Deanie which was chilli con carne, was now pebble dashed all over her wall and carpet. She did not look happy but cleaned it up.

The next day I awoke with a thumping headache. I looked around and could not see Ellie I instantly panicked, I ran downstairs and there she was eating her breakfast with Aunty Deanie. She smiled and said say hello to mummy Ellie. She smiled as soon as she saw me and I kissed her, trying not to look at her breakfast in fear of throwing up. There is a strong pot of coffee on and some paracetamol on the kitchen table, I kissed her cheek and said thank you. She told me to go back to bed and that she had everything under control. I did, it was nice to have a break and let someone else worry for a change. We went for a walk.

I was due home the next day and she asked me about my illness and Mark, I did not know what to say to her, I told her the separation was just a temporary thing, and that it would soon all be sorted out. I did not know if I was trying to convince her or myself. On the train, she waved us off with a tear in her eye kissing Ellie millions of times, and telling me how beautiful my baby was. I hugged her and thanked her for taking care of me. She gave me some money, and told me to treat myself when I got home. I slept on the train as did Ellie; I was shattered and glad to be going home. When I got in, mum had been and cleaned up for me, and there was a note attached to a big metal pan, with 'scouse and dumplings' love Mum. She had cooked my tea and cleaned the house for when I got home. How does anybody cope without his or her mum? I wondered.

I rang her and told her all about the throwing up incident. 'oh Grace ye never' I think she paid loads for that carpet as well ya know' nice one mum I thought, I already felt bad about it and embarrassed, we did both laugh a little though. Mark came to see me and Ellie he asked if he could take her for a walk, I was thrilled yeah that's great' I said ill just get my coat' she was 8 months old and we had never taken her out for a walk in the pram yet. 'Ill just get ready' I said. 'Erm no Grace I meant can I take Ellie out on my own. I was crushed. Oh yeah that's fine okay I said, let me just get her coat on and stuff. He picked her up, and walked out of the house pram in tow. I had used to it just being me and her, and it seemed strange her being with some one else even though it was her dad. He dropped her back off and said that he would see us soon.

Dave would come round and he would keep saying I am sorry Grace I never thought it would turn out this way. I assured him not everything that had happened was his fault. Carol and Dave would come round a lot, they were both good to me and helped with Ellie and if I needed anything, they were there. Nevertheless, it was different, it was not the same, they were like a second set of parents to me before, and somehow it was different, strained. Emma kept her distance she would ring and ask how we were now and again, but she was in to the party club scene and hardly anyone saw her not just me. Being the single mum meant exactly that, single and a mum. Everybody was there, when I needed them but I was lonely especially at night. I went from being in Mark's mums and being invited out a lot and being young to losing my mind, my fella and by the looks of it my life, nothing seemed to be the same.

I missed my old life desperately, I thought of Mark all the time, and how we used to be, and the agony of him not being here with me and Ellie was agony. Before I knew it, it was Christmas. My mum and dad always went away for Christmas, well since I was 17 anyway. I had always spent Christmas with Mark and his family. This was Ellie's first Christmas, she was 10 months old, and it should have been a happy family occasion. I did not know if it would still be appropriate to have Christmas there now, I wanted to be there but it had all changed, and Mark did not seem to want me there. Carol bought Ellie a beautiful dress to wear for the day, with a little hat, she looked so beautiful. She made dinner like she always did every year. Except the joyfulness of the whole day seemed forced. Mark hardly ate his dinner and before I knew it, he was out of the door. 'Where are you going' His dad said this is Ellie's first Christmas you should be here with Grace 'he said. Irritated Mark left. He bought Ellie lots of things but the thing he did not give her was his time. He said he would see me soon and left the house. Marks granddad was drinking whiskey and muttering under his breath' I don't know what's up with the lad' he said, if I was 40 years younger id marry ye me self he would say and give me a wink and a kiss. I felt lost, Emma smoked outside, she felt wrong smoking in the house and she knew her dad would not approve, she would hug me and sense the tension, and ask if I was okay, I nodded but I was not. I had shared so many things and made so many memories in this house, and I felt like I always belonged but today, I felt like an outsider. There

Was drinking and listening to old Christmas songs, while Dave made everyone Irish coffee. Ellie was shattered and had fallen asleep in her pram. I covered her up, and sat outside taking in the cold fresh air. I walked round the house, and found myself sitting in Marks bedroom, it smelled of him, and it made me remember when we were together, I felt close to him just sitting in his room. I sat on his bed, and looked around, it was a bloody tip, no change there then I thought to myself. I found myself wanting to tidy up, like I had done so many times before, but I never, I sat down again and looked at the pictures of Ellie that I had made for him by his bed, and the posters he had had on his wall when he was a teenager still there, old and faded. I could see a Kylie calendar baring her perfect bottom on the wall, and instantly felt intimidated by it. I Looked around I could see receipts for petrol, and half-eaten sausage rolls on the floor. What a pig I thought half laughing.

As I put them in the bin, I noticed a silver card on the floor, it was shiny, as I lifted crap off it to have a look at it, and it read: 'To my fabulous fella at crimbo' this card was not from me. My heart started to race, and I could not feel my legs as I opened the card. It read: To my gorgeous boyfriend Mark, has a good one I love you so much and will forever Cheryl xxxxx I did not even think about who the girl was, instead I sat hunched on the floor and sobbed holding the card. I cried more than I thought I possibly ever could. My sobs must have been loud as Emma and Dave came sprinting up the stairs. Emma looked shocked to see me so upset, and Dave just bent down on his knees and said what's the matter love? I could not speak; the sobs were thick and fast I handed him the card, curled up on the floor crying. He took the card and placed it on his bedside table, he didn't speak, he asked Carol to take me home, Ellie was awake, Carol said the sate your in I think she should stay here. I snapped loudly' no she is my baby and I want to go home I said as best I could through thick tears.

She helped me gather up her things and I went home. I was in a daze, this was my baby's first Christmas, we should have been together a family, and it should have been a memorable day. Instead, I was in utter despair, I was completely shocked he had met someone else, and I never thought it could be possible. I was heartbroken. I managed with all my strength to get Ellie to bed and asleep, I promised her it would all be okay in the morning. I sat hunched up and curled in a mass of tears on my old run down couch, and cried my eyes out like I had never cried before.

I must have fallen asleep, as I awoke to the phone ringing. 'Hello' I said. It was Mark. 'Why the fuck have you been going through my stuff in my room? How dare you go in my room why did you go in my room? I could not even say a word instead I just cried down the phone at him, I could not speak. Then the phone went dead he had hung up. I couldn't stop crying, and when I did, I wanted my mum, but I couldn't deal with her wanting to kill the man I loved right now, so I rang my best mate my rock, my Maria. 'WHAT!!!' she said she could not believe it, that complete and utter Bastard she said, holding back her own tears. 'Oh lovely ill be right round' within minutes she was letting herself in. She held me for half an hour and I eventually stopped crying. She made a cup of tea, and asked me to tell her what happened. I did, as I did this she stopped me mid sentence and said 'Grace what was the girls name on the card again' Erm Cheryl, I think why? She went white. Grace do you remember the girl who worked with him, who he used to help at college? Wasn't her name Cheryl? 'I dun no' I said why? I was completely dumb and deserved the title of dumb blonde.

Grace I would bet my house her name was Cheryl. Do you remember when you were pregnant, he would go out get all dressed up and go and see her and he would always be back late? She put two and two together in two minutes. As loyal as ever she said' im gonna rip her frigin face off' she said. I stopped to think about what she had said and the thought of him being with her while I was pregnant made me feel sick, then Maria stopped and said. 'Oh my god Grace I saw Mark, when you were in hospital, it was raining and I saw him in the car park of the supermarket, I walked over to say hello thinking he was by himself, and I realised he wasn't. There was a girl in the car, and something stopped me from going over and saying hello so I walked past and went to my car'. She said.

I could not stop the tears from flowing, I was hysterical, and I was so upset I made myself sick. Maria spent the night she held me and made me tea on tap. She was shocked and worried about me and felt guilt about telling me what she had thought, and if she had done the right thing telling me about the girl in the car when I was not here. 'Would you want to know' I said she thought about it for a moment and then said 'yeah I would'. 'So would I, I said through my tears, and she hugged me some more. I did not sleep; I tossed and turned all night, exhausted from my own tears and thoughts. I got up and rang his mobile. I withheld my number, and it rang. It must have been gone 1am. It answered. I heard lots of music, and people talking, I heard Mark say hello, and I lost my nerve and put the phone down. He was out clubbing it with his new trollop, I thought, I did not think I could cry but then guess what I did.

Chapter 18

HEARTBREAK

The heartbreak I felt was overwhelming, I was in so much pain, I thought I would die. I seemed to cry my weight away, and before I knew it, I was under eight stone. I was pale, and had black handles for the black bags that were under my eyes. I was 23 years old, and I looked about ninety. All the life that was in me, seemed to disappear. My mum wanted to kill him, she would cry along with me and when I did, she would tell me it would all be okay, but it was not.

Every time I thought about him with someone else, I wanted to scream but instead tears flowed and flowed. Ellie grew more beautiful by the day, and instead of enjoying her, I wasted the precious time crying for someone who didn't deserve to lick my boots let alone my tears, I just couldn't see what everyone else could, and as shocking as it was to me to hear of this girl, it didn't seem as big a shock as it was to other people.

I grew paranoid, and demanded that everyone tell me if they knew, they said they did not, and if they did, they deserved an Oscar for their performance if they were lying. I wanted to die. I rang everybody, to tell them I loved them, put Ellie to bed and kissed her gorgeous face goodnight. Got all my medication out of the cupboard, along with a bottle of Vodka, and decided Id had it, id had enough of my life, and this constant hurt and pain and I was going to end it all.

I took a few and swigged from the bottle, I felt sick; the alcohol was strong and stung my mouth. I began to cry; I raced upstairs with the rest of the pills and the vodka, and sat by my sleeping Ellie. I could not do it, I could not leave her. I decided that three pills and four swigs of vodka were not enough to finish me off and I rang Maria. 'What! "What the bloody hell are you doing"? "I'm coming round," she screamed in to the phone.

Within what seemed like seconds she was knocking on my door, she saw the state of me, and I crumbled to the floor. She sat holding me, and checked what I had taken. She raced to the bottles and made me promise never to do this again. What I had taken was safe, but to be sure, she made me make myself sick, she held my hair back while she did it. Crying while I threw my guts up. When I woke up, I was covered up on the couch and she was sat next to me with a hot cup of coffee. Throughout it all Ellie had stayed asleep. I did not want to die, I just felt so desperate, and so low and so heartbroken, I wanted an easy way out.

Maria kept an even closer eye on me after that, and it took a lot of persuading to stop her from telling my mum. I was quiet, I did not want to see anyone, and especially anything, that reminded me of Mark. He wore baseball caps, and I would see someone with a cap on and burst in to tears. I would see a car not even the same make, but maybe the same colour and I would be in floods of tears. I could be in Asda, and I would start crying and walk out. It was the worst time for me, and I hurt through and through. My CPN'S visits became more frequent, and she asked that I should get counselling, not just for the Post Natal Depression, but for my relationship breakdown also. I did not want to go; I wanted to be left alone. She put me forward for them anyway, and urged me to go. I said I would think about it.

I felt sick pretty much most of the time and it did not help by not eating properly. Dave and Carol tried their best to support me, but I knew they blamed themselves, it was not their fault, I think they thought because he had come4 home they were condoning his behaviour. I knew that wasn't the case but if you cant go home to your mum and dad when you did not love someone anymore what was the world coming too? I could cope with that, it was the him not loving me anymore that I could not cope with.

Dave and Mark began arguing all the time; Dave could not believe he could do this to us, to me, and to Ellie. However, he was his son, and he would stick by him no matter what. I knew in my heart when Maria had told me that she had seen him with a girl and it was the girl he would meet to 'help' (if that's what you call it) with college work, when I was pregnant, and the one she had seen him with when I was in hospital, I knew in my heart it had been going on for some time. But I just did not want to believe it.

I knew by the words in the card from this 'Cheryl', and I knew by the look on his face. His eyes could not lie. His Dad was so mad and would demand he see Ellie and help me, but the more he was told what to do, the more he rebelled away from his responsibilities and the situation. Not long after I had found out about the other girl, he moved out and he moved in with her. I was distraught. Everybody avoided telling me, but when they did, I was like a wounded deer. More tears I think everybody was sick of them by this point, including myself, but they just would not stop. I was completely worn out exhausted and tired of hurting. I had not heard off him for months and up to now, I had only received two payments of money from him. I did not want to ask him, but I was as broke as I had ever been. I just survived on what I did have, and sensing I was broke, Carol and Dave would leave money on the microwave or the table, or on top of the telly, knowing I was too proud to ask. I think in a way it made them feel better about what their son was not doing. Sometimes I would try to give it back, but they would not hear of it.

Maria would go through my cupboards and every payday she would fill up my cupboards and say; "now you can make me a nice meal"! She was great, and I felt so much better having her around. We had not seen Mark for at least two months, and then all of a sudden unexpectedly he rang me and asked if he could see Ellie. I did not even know where he was living with this girl and I did not know anything about her. I said; "okay you can see her here," "if you don't want to see me, ill go out so you can have some time on your own". I felt like I could not trust him, and I was silently angry he had not bothered to see Ellie for months. "Grace I am by myself ill only take her for a walk", and take her home, and give her a bath for you". "Okay" I said. I got her ready kissed her little cheek goodbye and off she went in the pram, it seemed so strange.

I rang Maria and she said she understood how weird it must have felt but that it was a good thing that he was making an effort with Ellie. He would not introduce Ellie to his girlfriend without asking you first, why don't you come round and have a cuppa with me she said. She picked me up in her little corsa, and she went in to the shop to get some milk, I waited for her, I looked up the road and spotted Ellie in her pram with Mark and a girl, she was pushing the pram and he had his hand on her back. I gulped hard, I could not believe my eyes, my heart started to thump, my eyes filled with tears, but this time I was not upset, I was angry. They looked like the perfect little family. I got out of the running car, left the door open, and raced toward the pram.

Mark stopped when he saw me, his eyes were as big as saucers, I could not stop the tears 'you're on your own are ye? It looks like it. Who is this Mrs fucking invisible? I was furious. Ellie smiled when she saw me, I touched her and said Ellie is coming back with me, I do not know this person and you lied to me. 'Don't be so bloody stupid grace I will bring her back later'. On first glance this Cheryl was fat, wore clothes that did not fit her properly, had long dark limp greasy hair, and had a face I wanted to slap on sight. She was smart, as she stayed quiet when she saw me. Mark walked away with Ellie. Maria came back to the car she saw the car door open, and the milk she was carrying ended up on the floor. She saw Mark walk away; she gave him an evil stare, and then scooped me up in to the car. "Come on grace". I sobbed and sobbed. Maria did her best to make me feel better but nothing did. It was gone 7pm and Ellie was not back, she was normally in bed asleep now. I tried his mobile and there was no answer, then a knock came to the door, he stood there expression less and handed Ellie over to me. "We have to talk about Ellie," I said in the strongest voice I could muster, but instead of sounding strong, I sounded like a weak kitten. "Yeah whatever" was his reply, and he left.

I put Ellie to bed and did not sleep a wink that night, I could not eat I was so upset, he didn't seem the Mark I ever knew, and I wondered if I had ever knew him at all. Seeing him walk down the street with her, with our baby, hurt more than I thought anything ever could. We were her parents, and we had never done that. I felt robbed and I felt like he laughed at me. How dare he not see her for months, and then lie to me about who he is with, and then dictate to me what will or would not happen with my daughter! He was manipulative and he could charm the knickers off a nun with one quick smile. He seemed to have everyone eating out of the palm of his hand. I am not going to be a victim anymore I said to myself.

There were weeks in between him ringing or even asking how she was. Then suddenly a phone call. Can I have El Today? "No you can't just be out of her life, and then turn up when you feel like", your mum and dad are having her all day Saturday you can see her then. Before id finished my sentence, the line went dead. That was how it panned out for a few months, when his mum and Dad saw El that was where he saw her. But his mum and dad were both managers, often worked at weekends, and were busy, but they didn't get to see her that often and when they did they would pop down to see her at home.

Mark was a coward he could not face me or face sorting out seeing Ellie with me. I did not want to stop him from seeing her, the opposite, but if something were uncomfortable, he would just run away and take the easy option. I learnt from Emma his sister that whenever her Dad and Mark were together they would argue and most of the time it was about me and about Ellie. Mark would turn on his heel and walk out, that sounded just like Mark.

I tried my best to get on with it, and the anger helped. Mum was having Ellie overnight for me, and it was nice for Mum to have some time with her, I walked to the shops and bought myself a magazine. I walked out and literally bumped in to a girl, I turned around to apologize and it was her. I froze, and just stared at her, she stared back, 'why you fucking looking at me Grace'? She said. She sounded so familiar. She knew my name. Then it hit me it was her, his trollop, Cheryl. How dare she talk to me and say my name, she sounded like she knew everything about me. I hated her immediately.

'What' I said. She pushed past me, she came right up to my face and said' Marks with me now so get over it ye sad cow, why don't you go back to your psycho ward' my face was red and hot with rage. I grabbed hold of her hair and threw her against the wall of the shop. She looked shocked and told me to let go. 'What did you say' I said "say it again". I was unnervingly calm. I still had hold of her. She screamed at me to let go. "I and Mark are together, and we are going to get married and have kids of our own so got used to it, and you can't keep me away from Ellie".

She said my baby's name and as she did, I saw a red mist wash over me; I gripped hold of her again. 'Don't you ever mention my baby's name again do you hear me? "She has nothing to do with you". She laughed at me right in my face and then said "you're pathetic", "I didn't have a baby to save my relationship"' "Ellie was a mistake".

The words hung in the air. I decided that was enough from this silly bitch and I smacked her as hard as I could in the face. She screamed the place down and people began coming over asking her if she was okay? Asking her if she was okay? I wanted to rip her smug little face off. She walked away and she got into a familiar car in the car park over the road from the shop. She opened the door of it, and I saw Mark, she got in and as she did she called me a "fucking psycho" and to keep taking my pills. The car sped off.

It started to rain; I dropped my magazine and cried the whole way home. It wasn't even 7pm I went to bed. I could not understand what Mark saw in this bitch, she was fat, I was no Kate moss like, but stood next to her I could have passed for a super model. She had a face you wanted to smack as soon as your eyes met hers, and the personality of a Rottweiler. I could have easily punched fuck out of the bitch. The psycho jibes and mentioning the hospital hurt more than I thought it would, but it made me realise Mark had talked about me to her, I felt like I had been knifed in the heart. It was like all the years of him being my friend, my lover, my Mark, it had all meant nothing. I felt heartbroken and betrayed all over again.

I picked Ellie up the next day, and told Mum what had happened, she was furious and she cried at the hospital jibes. 'Well suited if you ask me' "a bitch for a bastard" she had a way with words my mother. "Don't worry darling, don't listen to it, she's a silly little girl". "What goes around comes around eventually," she said. I went home, and the first thing I did was text Mark. "If that bitch your with, ever comes near me or my daughter again I will kill her". I pressed send and turned my phone off. He never rang me or text me again. (Well not for a very long time anyway)

The days turned in to weeks and before I knew it, everyday was the same as the one before. I would often spend days at my mums, talking and drinking tea, and trying to figure out what I was going to do with my life, but whilst I was figuring out what I was doing, I was being Ellie's mummy. I loved being with her, and I felt surges of love wash over me. I missed her when she was not with me, which was not often but when she was not I missed her so much. I felt guilty for feeling the way I did, but everyone kept reminding me it was not really me it was I but an ill version of me. I loved my baby, right there and then nothing mattered just her and me that was my world, and right then that was all I concentrated on, and the bond between us grew even stronger.

Chapter 19

JOB

I quickly got in to a routine with Ellie, and before I knew it, I was enjoying going to the park, taking her out for walks, and generally just being with her. She had a great routine at bedtime now and she would sleep all night for me. The house was as clean as a new pin, and things seemed better somehow. I was still desperately missing Mark and broken hearted, but I couldn't deal with it, I always said to myself, ill put it off till tomorrow ill think about it then, I would say this to myself everyday, not dealing with the problem or the hurt, I was too tired to cry anymore, so I thought id look at it when I was stronger.

It seems silly now when I think about it, but it was the way I coped. I could not fall to pieces anymore, I had El to think about, and I could not crumble. I found I was worse whenever I saw Mark's family, especially his Mum and his Dad, as over the years I had grown so close to them. Whenever I saw them, I would be fine one minute then just burst into tears. It was awful. I would see his friends; friends that I thought were my friends in the town centre, whom I had not seen since we split. They would always look at me as if I was some sort of victim or someone to feel sorry for. It pissed me off when they asked how I was, with this wounded look in their eye. I would smile say hello ask how they were and make some excuse with Ellie in the pram to get away.

I was skint. It is amazing how far you can stretch £40 a week, but somehow I managed it, but as Ellie was getting older, it was getting harder.

I decided that now that I was only on one set of tablets I was going to get a job. This did not go down too well with my mum and Maria; they thought I was rushing it. However, I thought no, I am sick of Living on benefits and having no money, I am going to get a job. I started to look, but then it occurred to me who would look after Ellie? I need not have worried my friend Pam, and my mum would look after her, until I could afford to get her in to a good nursery, and besides she was only 16 months.

Then the thought of leaving her hit me like a truck. Before I had even looked or gone for an interview, I felt panicky leaving her with someone else. Am I a bad mother? Will she forget about me? Will she think I am leaving her? All these things washed over me, so much so I decided I was going to forget about it.

Until the gas bill arrived. How bloody much? No, it was now or never. I had to do this. After having a chat with Pam and my Mum, it was decided Ellie was going to be looked after between the two of them, and I could try to start standing on my own two feet. I applied for loads, with Marias help, she would pick local papers up and take me to the job centre on her day off, and we would circle possibilities or maybes. It was harder than I thought. I applied for the job centre itself, the local vets working on reception, the local travel agents, and the Local council offices. I spent hours on my CV, and Marias dad Ted even helped me do a great CV to send in. I waited and there was no reply.

I felt upset and disappointed; would people want to employ somebody who had been sectioned? They did not know, I did not tell them, but what if it was on a database and people knew. Without me knowing? I thought. I carried on as normal, then one day Mum said to me, "Steve and Karen in the chemist were asking after you". I had not seen them since that fateful day it had all kicked off when I first got sick. I was embarrassed, and they were the last people I wanted to see. My mum said it would be nice to go in, say hello, and thank them now that I was on the road to recovery for all their help. I said I would when I had time, putting it off. Mum was going to meet me in town, to have a walk as she needed a few things and she thought the fresh air would do me and Ellie the world of good. She mentioned about forgetting to get something from the chemist. "Oh did you now" how convenient I thought.

I went in with her and the welcome I got was lovely. "How are you"? And he smiled a beaming smile at me. He looked at Ellie trying to pick up bottles of shampoo off the shelf and said how beautiful and big she was. My face was red I did not want to be there. My mum asked after his daughter and he said she had just found out she was expecting another baby. "Hasn't the other one just started school?" my mum said' "yes" he said smiling. "She must be gutted," I said, aloud thinking I was saying it in my head. The chemists went very quiet. It really was the wrong thing to say. "Actually it was a planned pregnancy" said Steve. I was so embarrassed I had said it. I apologised and ran out of the chemists. I knew what I meant in my own head, but it came out wrong it was never meant to be said anyway. I loved Ellie dearly and would be lost without her. However, being pregnant seemed like the worst thing that could happen to somebody, to me. My mum flew out of the chemists. "What déjà say that for" she said. I did not want to talk about and decided I wanted to go home.

I rounded the corner and began walking home, the traffic was heavy, and I decided to go over the zebra crossing. A car slowed down in front of me, and as it did, I realised it was Mark and Cheryl in the car looking at Ellie and me. My heart started to thump, Mark looked down, and Cheryl just glared at me through the glass. My throat tightened, and I could feel my eyes well up; I could not put this off until tomorrow I thought to myself. I just stood there frozen not crossing, and the car just drove off with her looking round to watch me as he pulled away. The tears spilled on to my cheeks and I wailed the whole way home. As I was getting to my road, Pam saw how upset I was and came racing over to me. I put my hand up and told her I was fine and that I just wanted to be by myself. She hugged me and said she would see me later.

I went in, and got Ellie ready for tea and bed like a robot. When she was kissed goodnight and tucked in. I sat alone in the dark on my crappy couch, and held my hands to my face and cried until I could not cry anymore. It was never meant to be this way I thought. I had pictures of me and Mark up, and realised the house was like a littlie shrine to him and me thinking he would come back. I was so angry seeing his little smug sexy smile looking out at me on the mirror, and with one quick swoop the picture was ripped to shreds. Funnily enough, it made me feel better.

I grabbed everything Mark had ever bought photographs, all his cards, and me I kept that he had sent me, and I made a bonfire in the garden. I poured myself a large glass of wine and watched it all burn. But it caught fire to the bush, and it spread to next doors! Oh no I cannot even get rid of stuff properly I thought. Then the bloody bin caught fire. The neighbours were out, and the black smoke filled the back streets of nelson road. The fire engine was called and soon they were putting it out. "You should be more careful next time you burn stuff," the fire fighter said to me, he looked about twelve. I nodded completely mortified. I decided I was going to bin stuff in future.

The next morning two letters arrived and to my surprise they were not bills, they were interviews! I could not believe it! One was for the Travel agents, and one for the vets. I did not have a suit or shirt and could not afford to buy one. I had ten pounds in my purse I decided to go to Oxfam and have a look. I looked and it was mostly junk, or clothes that my Nana would not even have worn. I looked through all the racks and I found a black skirt and black jacket the buttons had fallen off but they were originally from principles they were nice and did not look worn out, and were just the right size. £2.50 for the skirt and £3 for the jacket! Bargain. My mum sewn new buttons on for me, washed it, and pressed it, and I borrowed a shirt from my sister. I had tights and lent some shoes off Pam. I looked good in the mirror, a bit of slap and my hair done on the day and I could just pass for a normal human being I thought.

The day of the interview was awful, I could not sleep, I could not eat and I was so nervous. Everyone rang and wished me good luck, and off I went to the travel agents. I walked in and there was a girl with platinum blonde hair chewing chewy and popping it in her mouth. She looked late teens, and if looks could kill, I would be 6 feet under. I ignored her, smiled, and asked if the manager was around. As I said this, she came over. She was quite short with greying hair, but had a kind face; she smiled and held out her hand to shake mine. I did not realise it but I was shaking. We went into a room and there waiting for me was three other people. A balding man in a suit that looked cheaper than mine clicking a pen. A woman with a slight moustache that looked like my old headmistress, and a young woman dressed to the nines with three inches of make up on. I instantly wanted to be sick.

They offered me water and I said no. She then asked if I would like a coffee I said "yes" even though I did not want one, I did not want to appear ungrateful or rude. I had my CV and school certificates in a little wallet and placed them on the table in front of me. I could not stop my hands from shaking and I felt like I was having a panic attack. "Tell us about you" was the first question. My voice was shaky and high-pitched. I coughed and in my head I said 'come on grace you can do this, do it for Ellie' I waffled about where I had worked before, what my interests were and Ellie. "What do you think you could bring to the table if you worked here" the young blonde thing asked me. "Erm, erm, I am a fast learner and get on well with people" was my reply. They scribbled furiously on a piece of paper and they did not look happy. The stern woman then asked about my qualifications, I went through them and as I did this, a girl walked in with my coffee. I thanked her and she placed it on the table. I went to my little folder that I had brought and as I did so, I knocked the coffee with the side of the folder; it spilled forwards and spilled directly on to the young blonde things lap.

She was scalded and her elegant suit was ruined. She stood up and the balding man was trying to help her. She looked as if she wanted to kill me right there and then.

Even before that had happened, I knew it was not going; well I was too nervous I could feel it. The coffee had sealed the deal for them that either I was a moron or there was something wrong with me. I stood up and grabbed my folder, and said; "its okay ill see myself out". I got up and walked off. I could feel the tears stinging my eyes I felt like the biggest idiot in the world. I walked around town and I felt silly in my cheap suit. I looked and felt out of place. I looked at couples walking along, holding hands, and when I turned every corner, it felt like people were kissing. I felt like it was an epidemic, and they were waiting for me to see them for them to do it, to rub it in.

I remembered Ellie had ran out of calpol and walked to Boots to get her some more, while in the queue, I saw Cheryl. Could this day get any worse I thought to myself. She glared at me and I glared back. I could not seem to move without bumping into this cow. I almost wanted to leave in fear of getting upset and go to another chemist. However, I thought no, why should I? I have done nothing wrong i am not going anywhere. So I stayed put in the queue.

She looked at me like something she had stepped in, and I instantly wanted to smack her teeth in. Then I thought of her with Mark in bed, and her touching him, my face felt hot I was burning with rage and I had to move away in fear of hurting her. I was holding on to the calpol so tightly I was scared I was going to break it. I paid quickly and I could not help but hear her phone ringing. She snapped it open and I heard her say "Hiya babe yeah am just in boots wont be long yeah yeah okay will do love you" for my benefit I thought. It would have been so easy to throw her into the shampoo isle, straddle her, and beat her to a pulp. I could hear my heart beat in my ear, I was breathing hard and fast. I had to get out of this shop. I walked past her, and as I did I made myself not look at her, I thought if she looks at me in anyway that is not nice I am sorry she will get it. I was afraid of what I would do. But really it wasn't her fault entirely she didn't know me, she was just trying to hang on to her man (my man) he was the one who deserved a slap, I just couldn't see it, I was still totally in love with him, and missed him too much to realise what a selfish bastard he was.

I stalked home in the rain thinking could this day get any better. Everyone asked me how it went, and I did not have the energy or the shame to tell them I nearly gave a woman 3rd degree burns, I lied and said they offered the position to someone else. It really knocked my confidence and I decided I was not going to go to the next interview. "But you must go" Maria said. The next interview had been for the vets. I put the same suit on but did not wear as much make up this time. I had forgotten what wearing make up was like, it had been so long since I had worn it, being in the hospital, and make up was the last thing on my list of priorities. Coming home, it did not seem as important then either, but I made the effort anyway. I would apply it and then take it off; I looked like I had been tangoed. I promised myself that as soon as I had enough money I was going to buy myself some decent stuff.

Maria dropped me off on the way to work, squeezed my arm, and kissed me on the cheek. "Good luck darling she said' knock em dead".

I walked in to be greeted by a young girl on the counter, it turned out she was doing work experience from school, she could barely reach the counter, she looked as nervous as I did. I smiled a big smile at her and she beamed back. The vets were full with people, and animals. Dogs, cats, budgies, even a turtle. You could not move. The vet came out and as I was about to speak he said; "you will have to get in the queue" thinking I had a sick pet. "No I have c come about the reception job," I said. "Oh I am sorry" and he ushered me inside past all the people and animals. I was offered a drink, I shook my head no way was I going to attempt fate this time. "Have you had any experience with animals?" he said? "Erm no not really but my mum has dogs and always has had". I said. "Okay what about reception works"? "Yes I have got some I used to work at Crazy Georges the electrical appliance centre in the arcades". "Great" he said.

He was young and very welcoming, and he did not seem to have any airs or graces about him he seemed nice and friendly and I immediately felt at ease. He asked me some more questions and wondered if I was to be offered the position would I consider doing training courses on the medication for animals and to know a little bit more about my job. I nodded and said that I would. There was a huge gap in my employment history and he wondered what I had been doing in between. My mouth went dry, in my head I was saying, "oh yeah I had a baby, lost me marbles got taken away by the men in the white coats, and was sectioned for 6 months and the rest of that time i have been at home trying to get better". It sounded awful in my head so imagine what it would sound like escaping from my mouth. "I had a baby girl and I have been at home with her, that is the reason for the gap," I said. "Ah yes okay that's fine" he said and I left.

I felt it went well and felt more at ease then I did on the previous one. I went home not stopping to go into any shops. Weeks went by and I did not hear a thing, and then a letter appeared telling me it was nice to meet me but I had not been successful on this occasion. It really knocked my confidence. I carried on as normal looking after Ellie and that was when I discovered my love of books. I had all this time on my hands when she was asleep and I could not, and I would read endlessly. I always liked books at school, and I always read the odd one. However, because I was hurting so much, and found it hard to talk to people, I could escape in to my own magical world in a book. I read and read and read. One book after another, I could not get enough. I became a regular visitor at the local library, and soon I found I wanted more. Whenever I had any spare money on me or I dipped into my child, benefit when I could I would go to Water stones, Borders or even old book shops, you name it I went in. I loved looking at the books, new and shiny; it was like another world to me. Because I had my book to engross myself in, I didn't have to think about mark, it was easy to put him in a little box at the back of my mind, and leave him there and my tears until I finished a book, but when I did finish them I would read another one.

I read sad books, happy books, funny books, inspirational books, self help books, I loved this whole new world that opened up to me, and I learnt a lot a long the way. Maria came round a lot; she would laugh and say; "you reading again"? "Ye like a bloody book worm" she would laugh but pretty soon I got her into it as well. Then we would swap books. She would finish one and then come round for her next fix. It was then that I discovered Marian Keyes. I love her! Turning over the pages of her books was like having a chat, a laugh, and a cry with your best mate. I loved her books and I have read everything she has ever written. It would get me talking to people, if I could not have a proper conversation with them about me or life, I could always talk about books and what I thought of them, it was a great tool for running away from my problems.

Then one day a letter dropped, I had another interview for the local council offices. It was for the following day. I was shocked, but determined to go, and I did. I decided to take my medication in the morning of the interview instead of at night, and Maria joked and said; "they might think you're pissed"! I laughed as much as she but felt okay, and she drove me to the building. She was always there for me, and whenever she was near me, she gave me a glow and made me feel loved and made me smile. She was a great tonic to have around, and I felt very lucky to still have her in my life when so many other people had disappeared since I got sick.

I would tell her this and she would give me a kiss and say; "it would take a lot more to get rid of me that easy".

I had seen the building loads of times before passing going to the library, and growing up, but I had never been inside before. It looked huge and I wanted to run away. I was to go to the first floor, I was as nervous as hell. I went inside a cubicle, they seemed nice and polite, and all the usual questions were asked. I even managed to make them laugh! Alternatively, were they laughing at me? I could not be sure but hoped for the best. They showed me around the building and then where I would be working if successful. It was to be in the Housing Benefit section. I would not have my own desk. My title of job if successful would be 'clerk' I would be the one who maintained the huge filing room, and would find 'claimants details' as and when required. I would make the coffee and the tea in the morning and the afternoon for the whole office, and would do some data entry when people brought forms in from the counter. I would answer the phone and pass to the relevant person or take messages for them etc.

It did not sound like the highflying Melanie Griffith Working Girl job I thought it would be. I was a general dog's body a 'gofer'. Well that would do me if it means getting out the house and standing on my own two feet, I would do it. I could afford to get Ellie into Nursery, and with my Tax Credits I would get to top up my earnings and I could start to pay the debt off my mortgage off properly.

I could do this; I thought to myself it was not rocket science. I shook their hands and left the office, my heart beating the whole way. On my way out, I saw many people in suits much better than mine, waiting to go next for the same job, they looked older, smarter and better than I did. The confidence I felt suddenly deserted me, and I just wanted to get home and have a cup of tea and watch east Enders.

The very next morning I received a phone call from the Benefits Manager I had the job! It rang in my ears! I could not believe it I had gotten the job! My mum was ecstatic and so was Maria and we celebrated with a bottle of lambrini! We could not afford anything else, and Sue came over with a huge box of chocolates to tell me well done. Carol and Dave were glad and she said that Mark was pleased for me too. Just the mention of his name dampened the whole atmosphere, and I wanted to cry. How could I put him in a box in my head if people kept mentioning him? I had a job! Me! This was the start of me being me again, a new me, a better me, a better Grace.

Chapter 20

Making New friends

My first day seemed to be over in a blur. I got up that morning, ate breakfast, and realised it was only 5am. I had gotten up way too early, and I just sat on the couch and prayed. I prayed to god that today would be okay, and that somehow Mark would come back to me, and to Ellie, and my life would get better. Before I knew it, Pam was knocking on my Door. Ellie was dressed and ready to go, she would be having Ellie in the morning and Mum would be having Ellie in the afternoon. I would be home at 4.30 everyday. That seemed a long time to be away from her.

Pam was great, she was at the ready with toys and activities for her to do, she helped me so much, and without her and my mum, I would never have been able to have a job and support myself. I felt like a little kid in my cheap suit I would be the new girl. Pam picked Ellie up and told her to 'wave at Mummy', but she cried and kept pulling her arms out to me. I stopped and sat her on my knee, a huge lump welled in my throat and the tears were stinging my cheeks.

I felt so guilty for leaving her and told Pam I could not do it. What was I thinking of? I had missed so much already. Pam calmed me down. "Grace you are doing this for her and for yourself", "she will be fine" "all mums go back to work eventually". She will be fine and you will be fine, if she is not I will call you on your mobile straight away I promise. Ellie seemed to quieten, and Pam distracted her with a toy, while I sorted my face out. It was time to go, it was not far a 15-minute walk, but I was glad of the walk.

It was nice and fresh, and I thought about how different my life seemed now, and how much I loved Ellie, how much I needed Ellie as much as she needed me. This was the first time that I had gotten her back that I had left her in the day, and I felt like I was doing something wrong. The tears started again, and I decided I would not think about her, or I would be a complete mess before I even got there.

I went to reception and nervously told them my name and that it was to be my first day. Within a few minutes, somebody had come down to get me and take me up to the first floor of the housing Benefits department. I was as nervous as hell. I smiled, nodded, and walked behind the woman that was sent. Her name was Margaret and she was a Clerk like me and had only been there 6 weeks. I need not have worried about her she was lovely, and to this day is still a friend. She chatted about what Clerks do what are responsibilities are and where everything was. She got to the door of the office I would be working in she tapped in a number and said 'battle of Hastings' 'Excuse me' I said, she said; "that's the key number for the door" "1066".

We walked in and there were three rows of computer desks, all with people chatting and typing away on phones. There was a huge pillar, which stood to the side, and on it wrote, "You don't have to be mad to work here but it helps". Everyone looked up from there desks and Margaret showed me round.

Attached to the office was Fraud, and this office was much smaller with not as many people inside, but busy phones and computers buzzing. Everyone said hello and I was shown my job. I was in charge along with the other Clerks of maintaining the large filing room. It held all claimants old and new details. It had personal information and details of any Council Tax and Housing Benefit that had been claimed before. I was to maintain it, keep it tidy, and in numerical order. There were thousands.

It was my job to retrieve someone's file if one of the housing Benefit assistants needed it, and if it was not in the correct place it should have been, it was my job to find it.

There were also two huge tables at either side of the large filing room, where all the files that had been used needed going back. They were huge piles and I felt tired just looking at them. It was an endless job, as soon as I would start looking for files an hour maybe two would pass before I found them, then when I had actually found them I would have the task of filing the others away. That could take hours too. I would be on my feet all day; I was so tired from standing, but glad to be in work. My other duty was at 10.00am and 2pm making the tea! There was a huge urn and large teapot and a trolley. I had to collect everybody's cups, wash them, and pour tea. There had to be over 20 people in the office and they all had different ways of drinking tea, and some with sugar, some without sugar. Is this what I really wanted to do with myself? I thought. I immediately felt as if I was only good enough to make bloody tea! I got on with it, it could have been worse.

As I stepped out with the trolley, 'the hostess with the mostess' or in my case 'the stupid blonde who spilled tea all over the desks'. I was mixed up with the cups, and who took what sugar? And everybody looked pissed off. I wanted to run out the door I do not want to make bloody tea for loads of lazy people why do not you take your bloody cup and pour yourself one. That is what I wanted to say; instead, I cleaned up the mess, and felt like a huge joke.

Everybody in the office seemed to have a role, they knew what people were talking about on the phone, and what to type up on the pc, and I was the dog's body that did the crappy jobs, the gofer that made the tea. I felt so deflated. By the time it was time for me to clock off, I was well and truly knackered. I could not face the walk home and got the bus. I could not wait to see Ellie and raced to my Mums.

She was all excited to see me and greeted me with a huge smile, I was delighted to see her and smell her. I hugged her tight. "How was the first day"? Mum said. "In one word mum tiring". I told her I had the crappest job in the office. Mum as positive as ever said, "well it's a step in the right direction", and you can work your way up" was her reply. Right now, I want to have a bath and a play with Ellie and I want to go to bed, I thought and I did just that.

I got rid of the suit as I realised only the supervisors and Manger wore them. Everyone else wore trousers, shirts, and jumpers. I wanted to look like they did; I did not want to stand out. I promised myself when my first pay packet came I would treat myself. I enjoyed the job, as I did not have time to think, I could busy myself and not think about Mark or her, and I could get stuff done and then go. At first I kept myself to myself and hardly talked to anyone, I just wanted to keep busy. Then after a while some of the girls the younger ones like me, came and spoke to me. They were lovely. Laura, Catherine, and Jenny. They were the first sort of friends I made at work. They would go out every weekend and go to clubs and parties and

I was similar in age but with a baby. I did not want to go. They would ask every week and I would say no. However, when I have to know them a little better I decided why not? I should not have to skulk away and hide.

I went to a pub a local one and we had a drink, my tablets had changed and the medication I was on was very small in dose, and I could drink with them, but not too much. However, I was never a big drinker, always a bit of a lightweight, and I could not really afford to drink. These girls were similar in age but they had boyfriends, lived with their mums and dads, and did not have bills and babies. I always had to put money away to help with the mortgage debt, and to pay bills and provide for Ellie and me. It was hard, so most of the time I would stick to coke or lemonade.

After a while, I forgot about everything and enjoyed myself. I got on well with them, and they made me laugh, it was easy to be with them and I forget all my money troubles and worries. I worked hard in my job, I was getting a dab hand at the tea making now (not something to be majorly proud of I know) and knowing what everyone liked. I suggested after a few months, "why don't I pour the tea and ill take the milk and sugar round and they can have it the way they want it."

They were not happy at first, but after a while, it caught on and it was less for me to do, I had enough to do. I thought it was demeaning for me to make the tea anyway, why they could not get off their lazy arses and make it themselves was beyond me.

It was as if they were singling me out from everybody else. I did not want to make the bloody tea, but after a while I realised it gave me a break from the file hunting and welcomed it in the end.

I had been there a few months, I had not had any real contact with Mark, and he continued to see Ellie at His mum's. His Dad was mad about this, and told him he needed to take responsibility and move out, and have a real bond with Ellie. They got into arguments and he would do the usual when it got too much, he would just leave.

Because I was in work now, at the weekends I wanted Ellie to be with me as much as possible. So Carol and Dave would see me and her at my house, they would stay for tea, or take me out to give me a break, it was nice. Therefore, he was not seeing her much at all. He would spend most of his nights out with her, or with the lads, or at football, even his visits to his mum and dad would be short or not as often as before.

I still cried at night, and I would think of how it could have been. I was so desperate to touch him and see him smile at me, I was so stupid and young and in love, and the pain of him not wanting me anymore was too much to bear and most of the time I would go around with this hole in my chest that seemed to get bigger every time I saw him. I would pass him in the car and try to wave but he would look away or pretend he did not see his daughter and me. I would walk down the street in floods of tears. He started to pay me some money to help me, and I decided I would use all of that every month to pay the mortgage debt off, so it would disappear quicker. I had my wages to pay the existing mortgage payments, and all the bills. I would live off my child benefit and Tax credits. It was not much, but I got by, and at least everything was being paid. I was doing it by myself.

I started to feel better about myself, my confidence grew in my job, I was given training for the computer on typing, shorthand, data entry, etc and I ended up with a little more responsibility. I had lost so much weight and regained my shape I looked better than I did before I ever even had pregnant. With added stretch marks of course but nobody would see them.

I bought myself a few cheap but nice outfits, and I started to go out again. I talked to people and laughed again, something I had not done in such a long time. Ellie was two the time had flown by. I was a mother of a 2-year-old girl. Mark unbelievably had stayed with this Cheryl for all this time. Everyone including me thought it would all be a flash in the pan. He must love her, to stay with her I thought and the thought made me ache.

A lot of time had passed and it was clear he had completely moved on. But the ache and pain that he had left behind was still there for me. I was never the same as I was before, and I felt like I had been damaged. I did not ring him; I got on with my life desperately trying to forget him. Some days were easier than others were, but most of the time, the slightest thing would set me off.

It was nearing his birthday he would be 24 and since we had split up, I sent him a card off Ellie and me. We never got thanks, but it made me feel better sending it. I did not want to sit in on his birthday and think of all the other birthday's I had celebrated with him before. What could I do?

Then the phone rang as if by magic, it was Laura and Cath from work asking me if I fancied going out. Mum had Ellie and I tucked her up asleep in bed. I left mum with a DVD drinking tea, and her telling me to have a nice time. I had put on a nice dress, did my hair and left. We met in the pub, and then went on to a club that was local. I hated going to clubs loads of noise, and people pretending to have a good time, when all they want to do is flirt and cop off. I was not into it, but I went and had a few drinks and bumped into a couple of people from school. There first words would be "how's Mark"? "How's the baby"? I would shout over the music that I thought he was fine and we were not together, and that my little girl was 2 and lovely. It would always upset me the girls knew I had had too much to drink, and I began embarrassing myself crying saying how much I missed Mark and how Ellie didn't even know him and that it wasn't supposed to be this way.

The tears just streamed. I did not want to be here anymore, I wanted to be at home with my baby in my favourite pyjamas watching friends and eating chocolate. I wiped my tears away and Cath took me the loo's while Laura waited with the bags and coats. I looked in the mirror I looked like shit. My mascara had run my eyes were red and swollen and looking at myself made me want to cry even more. There were a big group of girls standing next to me, and I ignored them, I had suffered enough embarrassment it was time to go home. Cath had gone to School with Cheryl and she could not believe he would leave me and our baby for her. She had a reputation apparently and she was big and loud with a face like a smacked arse.

She soothed me and touched my face, "he's not worth it grace you are so much better off", "I know it hurts but it will get better". I held the tissue to my nose. "Will it?" Will it ever get better"? "It's been two years and I am still walking around with this hole this ache in my chest".

I broke down and cried while she hugged me. She went to the other mirror and I said, "Do you think he loves her Cath"? Then the girl stood next to me leaned over and said: "yeah he fucking does" "and I love him so get the fuck over it you silly bitch". I dropped my make up on the floor, my mouth was wide open, and it was she. Her words were like acid on my ears I ran to her and her mate ran toward me to smack me, and the other girl grabbed my hair. Cath saw what went on and quickly she grabbed the girl that tried to hit me by the head and slammed her to the wall. "And you can piss off this has nothing to do with you so leave it alone" she barked.

The other girl saw she was not messing, and turned on her heels. Some friends you have Cheryl I thought. It was just me and her and somehow we ended up in a cubicle.

I grabbed her head and hit her as hard as I could, the tears were tripping my face as I laid into her, then she suddenly got up and punched me in the face it caught the side of my eye. I lost balance and banged m head on the door of the cubicle. I started to scream at her and said "why"? "Why him"? "He was mine" "I loved him so much why him"? "You ruined my life" "I know that you were with him when I was sick" "I know you were" "how could you" "how could you"? I kept repeating myself and crying whilst I still had hold of her, she kept calling me names and struggled to get me on the floor.

The funny thing was I did not want to hit her, I just wanted her to feel something of what I was feeling, I wanted her to know the pain I was feeling, I wanted her to understand. The toilets had been cleared, and then the next minute, the next voice I heard was very familiar it was Mark.

He kept telling me to "let go of her" and grabbed my wrist, so hard I thought it would snap off. Cheryl stopped struggling as soon as she heard him and seemed to stop fighting. "Let go now grace," Mark demanded. I looked at him in the eye for the first time in a long time. "Do you love her"? I said, my voice was weak and my heart was racing. "Yes" "yes I do" was his reply. I let go of her and they walked out of the toilet. I fell to my knees and sobbed. I had gotten so low; I reduced myself to fighting with a girl in a toilet. I grabbed what dignity I had and left.

A bouncer came in, picked me up, and asked me if I was okay. He put his arm around me and said "he's not worth it honey" "you go home" and he escorted me out of the building. Laura and Cath were waiting for me with their arms wide open; they were waiting for a taxi. I dropped my bag and the kind bouncer handed it to me. "You don't seem the type of girl who gets in trouble," he said.

"It will all come clean in the wash" he said, something my mother would say I thought. He gave me a smile and walked over to the doors he was waiting by. In the corner of my eye, I heard his voice, Marks's voice. I saw her, and he was cradling her in his arms, there were clumps of hair missing from her head, and she had her arms wrapped around him. She looked like she was crying. I looked at her and him, they were a few feet away, she turned to me and she smiled the nastiest smile I have ever seen. Then buried her face in his chest.

I exploded with rage. I was scared at how much I wanted to hurt this girl. In that one smile, I saw her kissing him, and being in my house, when I was too ill to be there. I imagined her with my baby when I could not even be with her. I wanted her to feel a tiny fraction of what I had felt. I threw my shoes off, raced to where she was, and punched her as hard as I could. I grabbed her and started dragging her across the street. I wanted to take her somewhere and talk to her, let her know what hell I had been through. My head was fuzzy, she was kicking me and I gripped hold of her shirt I wanted to rip it off and shove it up her nose I wanted her to hurt, to hurt as I did.

But hitting her could not even come close. I let go, Mark screamed at me, I stood there and cried. They walked away from where we were, and I told Cath and Laura to leave, they would not. I wanted to be alone. The bouncer came, got me, and put his coat around my shoulders. "You don't give up you do you" "yeah I have now, I give up" "did I hear you've got a little kiddie," he said. Wiping the tears away, I said, "yeah she's beautiful" "déjà want to see". He put his glasses on, I nearly laughed it looked funny this huge scary looking man putting reading glasses on in the middle of the night outside of a club to see my little girl. He looked at her and said, "She's a little stunner isn't she" I smiled "yeah she is" "she really is". "Just like her mum", he said. "That's why you can't give up"

He waited with me and I had his huge coat round me, waiting for a taxi. The girls had gone, and he promised to put me in a cab. He did, he knew the driver, and said "look after this one mike" and he took back his coat. "You look after yourself love" and you look after that baby". "I will", I sniffed and wrapped my arms around myself in the cab. I went home and decided I had to let go, I had to move on. It was killing me being without him, but it was even worse wanting to change the past and the only person I was hurting was I. I suddenly wanted Maria and to tell her how stupid I had been. I did not go out for a very long time after that. The next day Carol and Dave had heard what happened from Mark. They took one look at my face "oh Grace what she has done to you" Dave looked like he as about to cry. I told them what she had said, but sobbed that it was my fault it was my own entire fault. If I had moved on, ignored her, and been a bigger person it would not have happened.

I had so much anger in me, and I wanted to release it on to her. As much as I hated her, it was not her fault; she was a silly kid in love with someone else's man. However, he was not my man anymore, and I had to get used to that or I would end up crazy. I had done crazy and there was no way I would end up crazy again. Dave listened as did Carol. He was mad; he said that she was not allowed in their home ever again. I said, "Dave it doesn't matter" all the fight I had in me disappeared. He was angry. I said I did not care anymore. "He loves her" "not me and there is nothing I can do about it". I wanted Ellie and nothing else I had given up just as he wanted he was free.

Chapter 21

COMING BACK

I threw all my thoughts in to Ellie and work, I saw Maria as often as I could, and we had a holiday to Ireland a two day break something we had never done together, it was great. Mum had Ellie and we ate out, danced giggled and talked as we did when we were at school we forgot we had responsibilities and houses. Maria lived around the corner from me with her then fiancé Karl. They had been together 9 years. Mark and I would have been together that long if we had still been together, I often thought about that, they had made it, but we had not. I shrugged it off I was not going to think about him anymore I was starting again the new me, the new and improved Grace!

The holiday was much needed and it was great for some girly time with my best mate. It was the first time I had ever been on a plane I gripped Maria's hand and she laughed calling me a chicken. We ended up in the Blooms hotel in the city centre of Dublin, nothing much to shout about on our budget but it was away from home, and we were excited by it all. Looking back in my head I thought people fell in love stayed together and got married. Simple. However, life is not, it is changing all the time without us realising that it is actually changing. I looked at my best mate and thought she had everything. My mum always says; "nobody knows what goes on behind closed doors". Moreover, it is true. My best mate, my Maria, was unhappy and did not realise it until she met her husband to be. She knew and he did instinctively that they were meant for one another, and that everything happens for a reason. Whilst I was concentrating on what I did not have, I forgot to look around at what I did have.

Time was passing and I still had this hope, this stupid hope that he would come back. I had to keep going. It had been months that I had not seen him for, but he was always there in the back of my head, and whenever I looked at Ellie. I decided I needed a change I was going to move house. I had paid the Mortgage debt off, and once I did, the four payments I received from Mark stopped. I did not want it, and he never got back in touch to reinstate it. I was standing on my own two feet.

I did peoples ironing for extra money, and did the Avon catalogue, all the pennies helped. I decided I needed a change too I was going to move! I started to do up the house and my dad and Dave, and carol would come and help hang paper and paint. I really got in to it, and soon the house looked great. There were lots to do, but it was getting there.

Carol turned up with more paint she looked odd. 'What's up' I said. "She said Mark brought me" "he's in the car waiting for me outside". I could feel my heart beat increase. I walked to the car and said, "you haven't saw your daughter in months", "look your with Cheryl, you want her, I get it" " but don't let Ellie suffer" "forget what happened and come in and see her you can come see her here anytime". He smiled at me, and got out of the car.

He looked around his old house it looked nothing like it did when he was here, and there was nothing there that said he ever was. He looked around in amazement. 'It looks great' he said. I offered tea and coffee and they stayed and had one. He tried to talk to Ellie but she clung to my leg she was wary. I picked her up and she played with the button that was on his jacket, he smiled nervously and said how beautiful she was and how much she had grown. He said that I was bringing her up lovely. It felt strange for him to say, as this was her dad. Nevertheless, I just nodded.

He left and as he did, he said; "would it be okay if I came here again". He looked almost apologetic. As much as I still felt all the feelings for him that I had always felt, I could not let that interfere with Ellie and him seeing her. She did not even know him, and that had to change. I did not want that cow anywhere near my girl, but if she were for him, I would have to let up on that at some point. As long as she was nice to Ellie and was respectful to me, if Ellie had a dad a real dad like she should have had from the beginning it would all be worth it.

I smiled at him in a way that said, "yeah you have been a twat" " and yeah you completely crushed me and our daughter" but I will let you try to make it up to her and to me" if a smile can actually say that, that's what I wanted to convey when I did smile. I told him it was fine to come on his own to begin with and we would talk about his 'partner' (better than bitch I thought) another time. As I said this, he frowned and said, "I want to see her without her if that's okay"? I nodded confused; I thought he would be delighted I was even contemplating it after everything that had happened. They had been together a good while now, I thought he would be happy I had involved her; it seemed to have the opposite effect. "Ring so you know im in, and if were not busy you can come up". He nodded and said thanks.

His mum squeezed me hard, and said "bell you later" with a huge grin. The next day whilst burning Ellie's tea, the smoke alarm was going off, and the phone rang it was he. 'Erm hi' I nearly choked on my own words' he asked how I was and asked if it was okay to call round. I had Ellies tea all over me. Within minutes, he was knocking on the door.

He walked in and I was 16 again. I was still completely irrevocably in love with him. No matter how much I denied it to other people I still did and knew I always would. I did not understand it and could not explain it, but I did, and it felt like a hundred horses were running through my chest. I had to keep this locked up and make an effort for Ellie.

He smiled, he was as gorgeous as ever, his eyes could melt me and I had to look away. "Accident" he said looking at my stained top. "You now me" I said, I smiled nervously. Ellie was asleep, great timing I thought, please wake up El and back me up, I thought. In my head, I was thinking, "why now El of all the times to be asleep you choose now"!

I offered him a drink, he accepted and I went to the sink to fill the kettle, there were plates and glasses on the drainer and I managed to some how knock them all off, there was an almighty crash on the floor. Mark raced to the kitchen, and I started picking the pieces up, and he bent down to help me. His face was an inch from mine I stopped and looked at him whilst he was not looking, he looked the same, he wore his hair the same, and I could smell his familiar aftershave. He looked up, and I looked away. I panicked and cut my finger on a piece of glass. It dripped on to the floor.

He grabbed my finger and held it over the sink under the running water. "That's quite deep" "you need a bandage for that," he said. We were standing so close we were touching. I had missed him so much. I desperately wanted to lean over and touch his face in my hands. Then I thought of Ellie he didn't want me, he wanted Ellie, that's why he was here, and for no other reason and there was no way I was going to spoil that.

She had missed her dad for too long because of the situation, I would stay away. As I was thinking this, he stopped and looked at me, his eyes were blue and intense I looked at him, and wanted to kiss him so badly. Then Ellie shouted 'mummy'. Saved by the bell or rather my baby I thought.

I thought I would pass out if my heart beat any faster. She ran to me, and held out her arms and saw Mark. 'Hiya' she said and Mark laughed. He touched her nose; she pushed her face to me. "She will be alright in a minute" "she will get used to you," I said. He stayed for tea and we chatted way after Ellie had gone to bed. We talked about the past, when we were kids, funny memories, and the time I nearly broke the cooker and hid it with the tea towel! And Carol went mad and Dave kept quiet about it for me.

We laughed and it felt so good, I had missed him, I had missed this so much and it was like it used to be.

I could feel the hole in my chest disappearing. He left and said he had had a nice time, and wanted to do it again. I said that when Ellie was more comfortable with him he could take her the park. He said that would be nice and we could all go. I meant just him and her; I was thrilled he had said it, but tried not to read too much in to it.

Even though the minute he was gone, I was on the phone to Maria dissecting the whole conversation bit by bit. That night I got a call from Carol she said that Mark had told her he had been to see Ellie and me. She was thrilled and asked what had happened. She said that Mark and Cheryl had had a huge fight about it, and he put the phone down on her, she had been ear wigging. I was excited maybe this was he realising that he had made a big mistake, and he wanted me back.

I could not sleep and I could not talk to anyone about it other than Maria. He came regularly and Carol had told me that they had spilt up she found her hammering on the door demanding that he speak to her. She was beside herself crying hysterically. What goes around comes around I thought, but I felt sorry for her too.

Mark never spoke to me about it, and I decided I would ask how Cheryl was? "We split up" "it wasn't working" he said, "It should never have been going on for as long as it did". I felt angry with him for discarding her as he did with me, did he have no feeling?

I walked in to the other room, and he sensed I was not okay. I was wondering when my anger would rear its ugly head, I had so much to say to him and I did not know how it would come out. He followed me in to the kitchen; he asked if I was okay. I turned around to look at him and said "you broke my heart" "and you were not there when I needed you the most and you left me" I did not realise I was shouting it I needed to say it.

He looked at the floor then at me and he said, "I know im so sorry" "that's why I stayed away" "I couldn't face you". "Please don't take it out on your daughter because you can't face me". I got upset and he put his arm around me. I did not want his arm there, which surprised me, he moved away and then I went to walk past. He grabbed my arm as I did and he said right to my face. "I do care ye know" "I might not act like it at times but I really do".

I looked at him and the tears were welling up, I put my arms around his waist inside his coat that he was still wearing, he looked uncomfortable and then that made me feel uncomfortable, I let go, said sorry and I walked to the living room, he came after me and said "Grace im sorry, I don't know what to say". He sat on the couch and I leaned across him. "Neither do I?" I said, and I leaned in and kissed him full on the mouth. I do not even know where it came from. He stopped and stared at me mid kiss, he felt warm and familiar and soft I needed him to touch me, and feel his arms around me. I pulled away. "I'm sorry ill get off" he pulled me back and said "no" "it's okay".

I sat on top of his lap and kissed him again and again, Ellie had fallen asleep to her Bob the Builder video, I stopped suddenly and felt guilty, I went to check on her, I covered her up with her blanket. I felt embarrassed being like this with him, this man whom I had known since I was 12, who I fell desperately in love with at 16, whom I bore a child too, it didn't make any sense. He patted his lap for me to come back I did, and then I suddenly remembered I was not wearing any make up, I told him so, he laughed and said "you don't need any".

We kissed more; I kissed his neck, and his face, and pulled him closer to me. It had been so long to see him, to smell him, to touch him. "Touch me" I said, and felt embarrassed by my directness. He slid his hands under my top, and I could feel his warm skin against mine. Ellie awoke and we stopped, he left not long after, then I thought I had made a big mistake I should never have done this. He did not want this. I did not know what to do.

I did not hear from him for two days. He then rang me and said, "Sorry I haven't been in touch I have been really busy". I was as awkward as he was. "Its okay ive been pretty busy myself"

I lied I hadn't id been waiting by the phone like an idiot. Wondering what his next move was going to be. He came around the next day for tea with Emma his sister. "Oh god he has brought her coz he thinks' im going to jump on him," I thought.

It was nice she tried to make an effort with Ellie but Ellie did not know her well, as she had big gaps in between her seeing her. But she was trying I thought. She had a lot going on in her life I was told.

She tried to play with her, and turned to me and said; "she's gorgeous grace". I thanked her and they left. As they were heading out the door, Mark said, "Can I come back later" "Err Ellie will be in bed, but erm yeah that's fine".

I could not help but be excited, I got dressed, and re dressed and put my make up on, I had a glass of wine. Ellie was on my knee and I was reading her a story she was tired, I put her to bed and cuddled her up. I must have fallen asleep I heard a bang on the door. It was Mark he had woken me up, I must have fallen asleep with Ellie.

I went downstairs and he was there at the door like a vision, my heart began to race, I felt like I was going to choke on my own spit. I smiled and opened the door "I fell asleep with Ellie," I said. He smiled, we talked and I made tea. There were awkward silences this time, and I kept making excuses to go out of the room. He followed me and I nervously handed him a cup. He took over and said ill make it, "okay" I said and he did.

I watched him in my kitchen, the kitchen that used to be our kitchen. It seemed alien after so long to see him standing there with the kettle I could not help but stare. We had tea and we talked about his mum and dad and many things then I mentioned the kiss, the little passionate kiss that meant everything to me. He said he did not know how he felt; I felt a stab of pain as he said this. I walked over to him and kissed him. I told him I was sick of pretending I told him I loved him even now, after everything that had happened I told him I loved him more than I had ever loved another person in my life.

I kissed him, he stopped mid kiss again like before, and said that he did not feel the same. I was heartbroken all over again. I said that I wanted him and to please make love to me one more time. I needed his touch his breath on my skin, I needed and wanted him more than I needed anything. He kissed me back more passionately this time. His mouth was on me and

I tore his shirt off with my hands. I kissed his body and smelled his scent; I kissed every part of him and made love to him like it had been that very first time when we were 17. I trembled next to his body. I lied next to him feeling his hot breath. He held me close and kissed me. He said that he had to go, I begged him to stay, but he wanted to leave.

How could he be this way with me and not love me anymore? I was so confused. I walked him to the door, he said he would ring me tomorrow and I closed it behind me slumping to the floor. Crying like I had not cried in a long time. I went to bed and I somehow felt dirty, like I had been used, it wasn't like before, it was different, I didn't know what to think.

He rang and said he had made a mistake, he did not feel that way anymore and it was time to move on. I was heart broken, I rang Maria and she was round in minutes. Hugging me as I slumped on the floor. He came round and I told myself I was not going to beg, I was better than that. He would come round and I would get upset and his arms were around me, we would kiss and then the next minute he would be ripping my clothes off and I would be ripping his off, we made love all the time, on the stairs, in the bathroom against the door, it happened whenever we saw one another, I felt sure he was fighting his feelings. Then one day he said I could not do this anymore.

I got desperate and panicked. I wanted to die; I felt like I could not breathe, it was like before except the pain was worse this time. Christmas time came round again, and he had a 'friend' a girl type friend, I felt so stupid. It turned out the reason he left Cheryl was because he had met someone else this 'friend'. I knew in my heart that was the truth as when he met her that was when it had all ended with Cheryl. I instantly and surprisingly felt sorry for her. I was invited to Christmas with his Nan and granddad and the family, and me and Ellie.

I could not eat I watched him leave with a stack full of presents for someone else; he left Ellie and me there, while he went and wooed some other girl. My voice was gone I could not speak; I shook as I watched him leave in the car. Nan and Granddad tried to make jokes with me, as Did Dave, I started to sob heavy loud sobs, Nan and Granddad looked at me shocked, Carol started the car. "Maybe we should get you home," she said. I cried in the car and she did not say a thing.

Everyone knew but what could they say? I arrived home, I just wanted Ellie, and to be by myself. I tried to contact him there was no reply. His mobile was constantly off I gave up. He did not visit anymore and he did not see Ellie either, this was my own entire stupid fault. I went back to work heartbroken.

I stopped talking, I could not speak; it was like the life had been knocked out of me. All over again. Weeks passed and Carol and Dave did not know what to say to me. They had been to Greece and this had all happened while they had been away, I tried to talk to Carol, but she didn't want to know, she didn't want to know the truth, she didn't want to see the pain in my eyes, I didn't tell her what had happened between us even though I desperately wanted too. I went to work, like a robot, days and weeks passed in to a blur. Everyone at work asked how I was I did not know what to say, I did not know what to do. So I did nothing.

Chapter 22

I'm Pregnant

I was like a broken shell all over again. It was my fault. I should have stayed away, he made it clear how he felt, and undying love was never mentioned. It was my own entire fault. With what had happened, he stayed away from Ellie. He never tried to see her or speak about her with anyone. I was beside myself. I went to work as normal and hardly spoke to anyone. Everyone noticed I was not myself, but nobody dared to speak to me about it. I tried desperately to immerse myself in work. One day I felt sick, I thought I was going to puke, I never made it to the loo, I threw up in the filing room I was mortified. I was sent home.

It got worse, I felt like crap, and looked like crap. I went to the doctor, it was confirmed I was 6 weeks pregnant. I collapsed on to the floor. This was the worst thing that could ever have happened. What if I had what I had before? What if I grew sick? Who would look after Ellie? All these thoughts raced through my mind I sobbed in front of the doctor "I can't be pregnant" "I can't" I pleaded. It was hopeless I was. I walked home in a blur. What was I going to do? All the things that could happen seemed to preoccupy my mind. What about Ellie? Was all I kept thinking?

I could not be out of her life for 6 months if I got sick. I felt sick I did not know what to do, or where to turn. All I kept thinking was they will think I Planned it' they will all think I did this on purpose, to trap him. Which couldn't be further from the truth? He did not want me, the last thing I wanted was to find myself alone again with two kids, and I did not want my little girl being without her mummy.

For a brief second I thought of abortion, and as the thought came, it passed me straight away. There was no way I was going to have an abortion, I did not want this baby but I could not do that. How was my life such a mess? I needed Maria, I needed to talk to her, I rang her number and she answered. I could not tell her; instead, I just laughed down the phone and talked to her like I normally would. I could not face people's judgements, not hers, what she thought of me was so important. I could not listen to; "how could you be so stupid" I was stupid more than stupid. I said nothing. She talked and talked, my eyes filled with tears as I listened, I could not tell her I could not tell anyone. I was ashamed of myself and my actions had cost Ellie her dad. I blamed myself, and that was bad enough I could not deal with other people blaming me too. If I blocked it out and did not think about it maybe, it would go away.

I could not sleep, I did not know what to do, I could not have a baby, no way, not with what had happened with Ellie, and not knowing there was a possibility that I could get postnatal depression again. How could I have been so stupid?

I tossed and turned all night, I really wanted to talk to my mum, but I just could not. I could not see that look in her eye and see that worry. I wanted to tell Carol but she had been so busy lately with work and I had hardly seen her. I felt alone.

I decided I was going to see Mark. I rang the house and got no answer. I picked Ellie up from Nursery and walked all the way in the pram. I was glad of the Walk, as I was figuring out what to say. I got to the house, Ellie had fallen asleep, and it began to rain so I pulled over the hood of her pram. I stood there frozen thinking of all the words I could think of to say to him. I took a deep breath and started to walk toward the house, when he came out of it, with a girl, a young pretty blonde girl.

I wanted to choke. 'I I' I 'really need to talk to you' I said in a weak voice. He turned to me and the girl got in the car out-front looking at me expressionless, and then looking at the pram as she got in. He walked toward me and said "can't you take the fuckin hint" and with that he got in the car and drove off. He left Ellie and me at the kerb of the road by his mum and dad's house.

The tears filled my eyes immediately. He was not my Mark anymore he was some horrible bastard that I did not know anymore and I was crying for some lovely lad that did not exist anymore. I sat on the kerb digesting the whole nightmare. What was I going to do? I was petrified, and alone. He did not want to know, and I never even got the chance to tell him.

I walked home and as I did the tears stung my eyes, I was lost, alone, penniless, and pregnant. I cried harder than I realised, and after a while, I passed three workers working on a road. They stopped and looked at me. "Are you okay love"? One of the men asked. I stifled a sob and said, "Yeah am fine" "really am fine" and began crying again.

They let me pass and the walk calmed me down, Ellie slept the whole way. I got in and sat on the couch I had decisions to make but I did not have the first clue how to deal with them. I rang my mum and cried down the phone she was instantly worried and wondered what was wrong, I made up an excuse, I needed her and I needed her ear and her comfort even if it was a lie. I fell asleep that night thinking of all the possible outcomes. I woke early and decided I had made my mind up. I did not intend on getting pregnant, and in no way wanted, what happened with Ellie to happen again, but there was no way I could ever abort this baby. This was Ellie's sister or brother whatever the outcome, I was going to have this baby. I promised myself I would wait until the 12 weeks to tell everybody, including Mark, he did not want to know but I had done a good job with Ellie I would be okay. I was trying to convince myself, and then in the time I had to wait for the 12 weeks to be up, I could get used to the idea and then it would not be so shocking.

I went to work as normal and did everything the way I normally would. But I felt as sick as a dog. I pretended that I had caught a bug and that was what was wrong. A few weeks passed and I was terrified of what was going to happen, but I knew this baby must have been sent I had to have it. I loved Ellie and this was her brother or sister I could never not have it, I seemed to convince myself of this thought every time it passed my mind almost trying to convince myself that I was doing the right thing

One day I went to work as normal I filed files away, and chatted to the girls then the next minute I felt a stabbing pain to the right side of my body, it was agony. I dropped a file and lurched forward on to the floor. Luckily, there was no one around. I hurried to the toilet, and then there was blood. Thick mass of blood between my knickers part of it was black. My stomach ached I writhed in agony. There were people in the loo, so I tried to stay quiet. I could hear muffled voices talking about nights out and what dresses to wear. I desperately wanted to go home. The Pain got worse and felt the blood trickle between my legs. I started to cry. I heard one of my friends in the loo. I shouted out to her and said; "please get my hand bag, and coat and tell work I must have caught a bug I need to go home". She answered me from the toilet asking me if I was okay, I said "yeah fine" in the lightest voice I could muster. True to her word, she came back, with my bag and coat.

I scurried to the door once she had left and waited for the toilet to become quiet. I left and clocked out. I walked to the doctors, which was round the corner but seemed like an age to get too. I spoke to the receptionist in low whispers she nodded and with what seemed like minutes I was being seen by a doctor. Not my doctor but a doctor .I saw the nurse and explained how far gone I was, she examined me and then asked for a doctors second opinion. She told me I had miscarried my baby. I did not want this baby in the first place, I should have been glad but I was not.

I started to cry and sob aloud. The nurse put her arm around me and told me it was going to be okay. I felt like it was my fault, my baby this poor thing had died inside me. I felt like I was going to burst. I could not tell anyone, I could not deal with anyone's judgments right now. I cried solidly for hours. Then I realised the time, it was time for me to pick Ellie up. I got up quickly and left. The nurse handed me a card and asked me to come back. She said that I had passed the baby and to come back to check I was okay. She gave me a pad and a number and I left. That was it. A life over in half an hour. I never wanted to get pregnant and I did not want this either, the situation had been taken out of my hands now.

I picked Ellie up, and beamed at her, she was happy and cupped my face and said "Mummy" repeatedly. I was so happy to see her. The staff told me what kind of day she had. Mum and Pam had told me how great the nursery was and she had eased me gently in to believing it was better than what her and mum could offer, I wasn't so sure at first, but as ever she was right. It was the best move I had ever made. Ellie was bright and learnt so many new things the nursery was amazing. I walked home bleeding all the way.

I got home and as if on automatic pilot, I carried on as normal. I read Ellie her book, tucked her in bed, and started a bath. I took off my bloodstained knickers and looked at what was left of my baby. I couldn't stop crying, how could I have been so stupid? How could I have let this happen? Carol came the next day, I wanted to talk with her but I just could not, I could not face anyone. I decided I was never going to talk about it. Therefore, I kept quiet. She noticed my mood and asked if I was okay, I nodded and we carried on talking, as we would have always done. I was never the same again, I was like a hollow shell, I could not be me again, and I just wanted to run away. I carried on like this for a long time, and after a while, I almost believed I was doing okay, even though I knew deep down in my heart I was not.

Months passed and no news of Mark. I had not heard from Carol or Dave in ages I was starting to worry. Then out of the blue, a phone call from Emma Mark's sister .She told me that Carol had left her dad. I nearly dropped the phone. What? I shouted down the phone, I could not believe it. "Why" was my first question? Emma sounded like she was going to cry. "She's met someone else." I was dumb struck. Whilst Dave was at work, she packed all her belongings and left. He was heartbroken. I rang him immediately wondering and worrying how he was. His phone went on to voice mail. I did not know what to say or what to do. I asked after Mark, she said he was okay, and she quickly got off the phone. "Mum will be in touch," she said and with that, she hung up.

I was so shocked. They had been together since they were 15. I tried to ring her, but her mobile rang out, I was so worried and I was glad not of the situation but of the distraction it gave me to my previous predicament. I managed to speak to Dave he was utterly heartbroken he sounded like a broken man on the phone, and I did not know what to say to him. I told him I would come see him with Ellie, and he seemed pleased by this. A few weeks passed and out of the blue Carol rang me and told me she wanted to see me. I was so relieved to hear from her, she was all right. She pulled up in the car outside and her man was waiting in her car, she asked if he could come in, I said no. She seemed put out and I did not explain any further.

"I wanted to tell you" were her first words, she started to cry, I put my arms around her, and hugged he, she looked so lost and broken, a bit like how I felt but for different reasons. Ellie smiled at her sitting by my legs playing with her plastic animals. With everything that had happened, Ellie or me had not heard from anyone it had been weeks without contact.

So Ellie was strange with her, I think it upset her. I listened to the story of how it all happened but I did not feel comfortable with her man sitting in her car outside my house. I was glad when she said she would not stay long, I felt awkward and I felt like I would hurt Dave letting him in. I didn't want to get involved I just wanted to know that they were both okay and Emma and Mark were okay Carol said Emma was finding it hard to talk to her, but they were talking, but Mark did not want to speak to her at all. She cried as she said this. "It will take time" I said "let them get used to it" and get over the shock of it".

Emma had told me how she left, I could not sit there and pretend what she had done was all great and rosy I had to tell her, I had been apart of the family too long to sit and say what she wanted me too. "The way you did it was awful Carol" "you sneaked off took what you wanted while he was in work and just left no explanation anything", "you didn't even tell him to his face".

She nodded with me and said it was a coward's way to do it, but she said if she had seen him, it would have been harder to go. I felt sorry for her, as I did for the whole family. The family were gunning for her. Her kids did not want to know her, but I felt disappointed in her, almost ashamed. I had known her since I was 15, her opinion and values meant a lot to me, I felt like I did not know anything anymore.

She hugged me, and she said once she was sorted properly with somewhere better to live she would ring and we would meet up. I agreed and watched her leave with the strange man in the car. I felt a pang of hurt seeing her with him; it was as it was my own mum and dad splitting up in a way I felt like one of the kids.

I shut the door I could not digest what was going on. I rang the house to check Dave was okay, Mark answered the phone, and I had not spoken to him since that day, that he told me to fuckoff. So much had happened since then. I swallowed hard. "How are you"? "Fine"' he said, "how's your dad"? "Not good to be honest Emma is staying here she doesn't know what to say to him"." Have you heard from your mum"? I did not want to let on she had just been here to see me and Ellie encase she could not face him. "No" his voice was cold and hard. I knew he must have been going through pure hell, I hoped that the girl he was with was being there for him, knowing Mark he would be suffering in silence.

"Did you know Grace" he asked, "Mark I didn't know a thing until Emma told me, I swear". He said he had to go and passed the phone to his dad. He sounded terrible. "I've done all my crying Grace," he said "ill be okay". I told him that I loved him and so did Ellie and he could come see us whenever he wanted. We arranged we would meet up the following week. He looked a wreck when I saw him.

I wrapped my arms around him and gave him a big kiss on the cheek. We talked a lot for at least an hour about various things. You are not meant to have a favourite in a family especially your ex's family but when we were together his family were like my family. I loved Dave to bits, he always saw my point, and was protective and loyal and loving and never left me or Ellie out, we laughed a lot together and he was just like another Dad.

It was so good to see him and be with him even if it was sad. It became a regular thing him coming for tea say once a fortnight or so as he was busy working mostly and I would pop round and see him. Carol had sorted a place in Manchester and I met her new man. He was not Dave and I did not approve of what she had done, I decided I was going to have an instant dislike to him. It lasted all of five minutes he was a lovely person. He fell in love with Carol and he wanted what was best for everyone Dave included, he seemed to care a lot about what had happened and he tried hard with me and with Ellie.

I liked him but I did not feel comfortable liking him, I felt disloyal and I did not feel comfortable with him straight away. A few weeks passed and we hardly saw anyone, Ellie and me.

We saw my family and every now and again Carol and Colin would pop in and have dinner, and Dave's visits became less and less. We spoke more on the phone. Ellie had not saw Mark for over 6 months, he was not helping financially or being any type of a dad. From when he left when she was 6 months old, I could count on my fingers how much time he had actually spent with her, it did not amount to very much and she did not even know him. I decided I had to ring him I had to speak to him solely about Ellie. I wanted her to have a dad I was still hurting over everything, and I didn't want a strange woman being with my daughter but if we did it properly and be grown up about it, I would let them both come to the house and as hard as it would be to see them I knew I had to try at least for Ellie. I could not look her in the eye when she was older and say I did not try.

I dialled his number he answered and realised straight away it was I. "Mark listen I am not ringing about your mum or your Dad I am ringing because I want to know if you want Ellie in your life"? "If you do I want to make it as stress free as possible on all sides but if not id rather you stay away for good and not pop up when you get bored or are curious". I said it, I said what I wanted to say and I did not get upset. I took a breath he said: "Grace I'm driving ill have to ring you back". That was the last time we ever spoke on the phone. He never rang back. I deleted his number I give up.

From now on, it was I and it was Ellie, I was and always had been a Mummy and Daddy in one, and she was smart, funny, caring loving and she was beautiful and she was all these things without him, we are going to be fine. I said this to myself repeatedly in my head I wanted to believe it.

Carol came for a visit with Colin, we had not seen her for a while, I let them in and made tea, they kissed me and sat on the couch. We talked at length about different things and what had been happening in East Enders etc general chitchat. Then she hit me with it. Mark and his girlfriend had a baby boy 2 days ago. I dropped my coffee cup and it smashed on the floor. I could not breathe I collapsed on the floor in hysterics, Ellie started to cry seeing me so upset. She tried to comfort me, I had to get out, and I had to go upstairs.

I cried and sobbed on my bedroom floor and I shook with pain. If I had of had the baby I lost it wouldn't of been that much older than this baby now. It may sound stupid but it was as it was my baby, and she had it with him. The more I thought the more I cried. I did not even know she was pregnant. Why didn't anyone tell me? I suddenly stopped crying. I had been a 'victim' for too long I was suddenly angry. I raced downstairs nearly tripping on the way Carol and Ellie were laughing on the floor with Colin; she looked up almost bored of my tears. "When did you find out" I snapped.

"Grace we didn't know" "he didn't tell anyone", "I didn't know". "What"? "Are you trying to tell me you didn't know your son was having a baby"? "Yes" "that's exactly what I am saying" "none of us knew a thing until Mark rang and told us he was here, we are all as shocked as you". "Have you seen the baby yet" "Yes I went to see him yesterday".

She sounded light and breezy like we were talking about opening a bar of chocolate. I was shocked at her coldness. She did not know about the miscarriage, and that made it worse, but it was as if Ellie and me never existed, we did not matter. This baby was Ellies half brother and I should have known. I was suddenly furious. "GET OUT OF MY FUCKING HOUSE RIGHT NOW" I had not realised I was screaming. Carol looked like she had swallowed her handbag, she was overcome and looked at me shocked and just sat there. "GET OUT" "GET OUT" "GET OUT" She was angry and started telling me to calm down this just made me feel worse.

I needed someone to hold me up, I needed someone to hug me, and tell me it was okay, I felt like I was going to fall over with grief. I felt like the stupidest person alive. Colin did not react to me, he leaned over and shushed me and grabbed me, I was grateful for the arms being around me. I did not expect this off a man I hardly knew, I expected it off a woman I had loved and been apart of since I was 15 years old. I got nothing but a look of disgust. I cried on Colin and said, "Can you please go".

He nodded and gathered his things up, Carol said; "I don't think Ellie should be left with you in this state".

At that point, I wanted to smack her in the teeth. "How dare you"! "How dare you even say that to me?" "How dare you Ellie is and always has been my number one priority". "Get out of my house". She walked toward me, she had forgotten to pick up her cardigan, I did not realise this, and screamed again "GET OUT" "GET OUT" "JUST GET OUT"!

She hurried and headed for the door. I locked it and sobbed. Ellie was sitting with her toys looking at me with a big lip wobbling, she looked like she was about to cry. She did, I flung my arms around her and sat her on my knee and we cried together. She fell asleep on my knee. I looked at her gorgeous face, and stroked it while she slept. I am only going to think about myself from now on my family is I and Ellie everyone else can sod off.

I felt like nobody thought about us on his side, I felt like we were the mistakes, and he was making his 'real family' now. I felt sick I wanted to throw up. Losing the baby had been a blessing in disguise, something I never ever thought I would say. It was I and my baby against the world. Suddenly it all made sense why Dave had stopped coming round. He knew about the pregnancy and the baby and he could not face me, he knew Mark would never tell me, did not want to be the one to tell me. A few weeks passed and there was a knock on the back gate. It was Colin, and it was not really a surprise to find that Carol had not come with him; Mark was definitely a chip off the old block when it came to being a coward.

I was pushing Ellie on her swing. He walked in with presents for Ellie as she was going to be four the next day. He put them on the floor, and smiled at Ellie then at me. "Hi" I said. Id had time to calm down. He was there to do Carol's dirty work as she did not have the bottle to come herself. All I wanted was an apology for the way that she had told me, and the way Ellie and I were not in the picture about anything.

This man was not Dave, but he was a nice man I had to admit that and he genuinely seemed to care and love Carol, he must have done to put up with the crap her family had brought her. I suddenly realised, seeing them all of them, his whole family was killing me, it was stopping me from moving on, being a mum that leaked a lot, and having no confidence. I could not have people coming in and out of Ellie's life all the time it was not fair. It was bad enough having no dad for her but everyone else following suit I could not do this anymore.

He started to talk about what Carol had said, and how hard it was for her to tell me etc. I stopped him mid sentence and said "I can't see her anymore", "not just because of that" "and the way she dealt with it all" ive realised I have to stop living in the past and move on like everyone else has been able to do". "I won't change my mind", "I can't see you any of you anymore", "and it's not as if anyone really bothers with Ellie anyway".

"I don't want to stop Carol from seeing her granddaughter but I have made a decision". "Carol's sister in law Wendy can pick Ellie up once a fortnight and you can have her for the whole day", "and then she can see her other side of her family and anyone else who wants to see her can see her then".

"Grace I don't think Carol will like this". "Tough I am thinking about me and my daughter and what's best for us". "I have spent too long thinking about other people". He looked shocked it was not in my nature to be like this. Id had enough I just wanted to get on with my life and bring my girl up well. I was tired of the upset I was tired of the crying I had no fight left in me. I wanted to be sure that they would all still see her, she was a good Nan and I wanted Ellie to have that and knowing Carol she would rally around the people that didn't bother with Ellie and make it a regular thing.

I thought she would be happy with this. Colin left, he rang me that night "she doesn't want this Grace" "she loves you too", "not just Ellie". "She should have thought about that when she didn't care for my feelings". My voice was cold. I did not cry I did not have anything left.

"She has said no to what you want to do," he said. "Fine if she wants to lose her granddaughter because of her own stupid stubbornness and self righteousness I won't hold her hand on the way down". "Look after her though Colin" "and whatever you may think I do love her", and I put the phone down.

I did my best I could not do no more. I did not ring any of them and I focused completely on Ellie we went away for a while to a caravan with my sister it was just what we needed. I managed to get my head together, and for the first time in a long time, I relaxed. Another month passed and I began to feel better about it all, I knew that I needed to get away from them all, it was destroying me and I did not want Ellie growing up with a nervous wreck for a mother. I knew I had made the right decision. It was better for Ellie to have people that loved her who were constant in her life than snippets of people coming in and out of it. Carol always saw her and Dave did when he could but things had changed. I gave them an option to see her and have a full day with her once a fortnight that could be changed to suit them if things cropped up, but it was rejected; it was as if what we wanted did not matter.

I decided that what they wanted did not matter and I was taking control. I knew in my gut it felt right, and I did not think for a second Carol would not see Ellie just to spite me or of fear of losing face, I awaited her call but it never came. It made me think even more it was the right thing to do. Then one day on my way in from work, I heard a familiar voice. "Hello babe" it was Dave. We had not seen him in ages. I flung my arms around him like I always did, and today he seemed to be stand offish, he hugged me, but he looked awkward and uncomfortable.

He brought a huge box, and many little boxes all wrapped up beautifully, they were for Ellie. They were very late birthday presents. "I am sorry they are so late love," he said. I put the kettle on. "Its okay" "you've had a lot on your mind". He did not look like the Dave I used to know, the beaming smile that was always planted on his face was gone, he looked tired he looked old. He looked in pain. He had big bags around his eyes and he looked like all the life had been taken away from him.

I hugged him closer to me, asking him if he had eaten, he said he was not hungry. Ellie wanted to be out in the garden and she was off putting her wellies on.

Dave stayed to talk to me while we watched her on her swing from the window. "What's the baby like" I asked. "I don't think we should talk about it Grace", he said. I agreed and I do not even know why I had asked. We changed the subject, I looked at the huge box on the floor it read "To Ellie have a lovely Birthday love Daddy" xxx My mouth flung open, it was from Mark, we had had no contact or financial help or even seen him for way over a year. He missed Christmas and then out the blue he gets his Dad to turn up with a gift for her that he couldn't even give her himself 6 weeks too late!

I was furious. "What the bloody hell is this"? Dave looked at the floor then at me. "Grace he wants her to have it" "don't deny her that".

"Don't deny her that"! "Don't deny her that"! I said the words again, but louder. "Are you joking"? "He has done nothing for our child" "absolute zero"! "He hasn't seen her when he could have", "I rang him about it" and he never rang me back"! "He turns up with this overpriced piece of crap thinking he can buy her off"? "Well when I say turned up; he gets you to bring it because he is such a bloody coward"! "Well he can stick it where the sun doesn't shine"! "Tell him to give it to his little boy he can go and play happy families with her".

I did not realise it but I was shouting at Dave. In all the years, I had known him we had never fallen out once. There were times he could have skinned me alive like when I accidentally poured coffee on his new computer when I was cleaning it, or when I dropped, a dish set on the floor in the kitchen that they were planning to take with them to a wedding. Not Dave, he would smile and say; "bloody hell grace" and help me pick it up, this time it was different.

He looked at me and said, "I can't deal with this anymore". I apologised for shouting and he said he understood but he was supporting Mark. "At least he was trying," he said. The more he said this, and defended him the angrier I got. "Please tell him to stick it".

He kissed El on the head and walked out. It was the first time he had ever not given me a hug or a kiss on the cheek goodbye and then he turned and walked away. I felt hurt, it was the first disagreement that we had ever had. I did not realise at the time that would be the last time I would ever see him.

Chapter 23

DEATH IN THE FAMILY

Life was good, it was me and Ellie and I started to laugh again, and feel better about myself. Ellie was settled and had started school, she loved it, and her teachers loved her. 'Very intelligent' 'knows her own mind' "but tends to chat a little too much" I read in her first school report. I laughed when I read this. She was so like me! She was doing well and settling in.

We had moved house, and it needed doing up. I made some money from my two up two down and Ellie and I went away to Wales just me and her it was fabulous. We went swimming, went to a kids disco, horse riding, she didn't want to come home. Overall I felt better. I had made so many new friends at work, and of course as ever Maria was always there. She would come down and scrape the wallpaper off with me in the hall. There was so much to do, I couldn't stand that bathroom.' "Its chintztastic"!!' Maria would say and laugh. I bought the house initially to do up and make money on so when Ellie got a bit older we could move to a better area. This area wasn't ideal, but while she was small it would do for now.

It was huge compared to my two up two down, and I loved the fact that I walked into a hall, not directly into my living room. This house was a new beginning for me. It was completely ours, mine and Ellie's and nobody would interfere with that, and we could make new memories and start again a clean slate.

I became really good mates with a girl at work called Kerrie, she was lovely, we got very close and we would often sit together at night over a few glasses of wine wondering where it had all gone wrong, and why weren't we happy and married? She would make me laugh and she had this warm glow around her that seemed to pass to me whenever I was round her. She was a joy to be near and I lover her dearly.

She had been in our place a while and she got on well with everybody. She was single with no commitments and so was another girl in the office Louise. They decided they were going to Australia to travel for a year. I was shocked and a tiny bit jealous if I am honest, I had commitments, I had Ellie, and she came first, I was going to miss her more than anything else.

She packed up and off she set, crying as she went. She would ring me all the time and send lots of lovely postcards Ellie adored her. We both did, I missed her so much.

I was late one day for work running round like a lunatic one morning trying to get dog poo off Ellie's school shoe. The phone rang It was Kerrie. "Hi I said sorry Hun I really want to hear all your news but I am late for work and Ellie's late for School"! "Have got dog poo all over my"... "Grace Stop". She sounded different.

"What's up Hun" I said "sit down" "I have got some very bad news you". She said." What" "this didn't make any sense"? How could she have bad news for me she was in Australia?? "Is this a joke Kez"? "Grace no its not" "you don't know do you"? "Know what"?!! "I knew they wouldn't bother to bloody tell you".

"You're scaring me please tell me what's up"? "Sit down" she said again. "No I am fine".

"Grace Dave has died". "What"? The only Dave's I knew were Marks dad and his Granddad. "Oh god has he?"How do you know"? Her mate Keeley lived across the road from their house and she heard and sent Kerrie and email asking how I was.

But Marks granddad lives in Eastham? I said very upset but confused.

"No Grace I mean Dave, Ellie's granddad Dave". I dropped to the chair. "No 'Kerrie your mistaken" "he's only 49 he is fine we haven't spoken but he is he is fine he's at home now you're wrong"!' "Grace I wish I was, "I am so sorry I knew how much you loved him" "Kerrie they would tell me"!"This is a big deal I am telling you all the years I have been part of that family they would tell me"! "He is Ellie's granddad for god sake".

I didn't believe her, I got Carols number out my bag and asked Kerrie to please ring me later I think there has been some mistake, and I am going to ring Carol. I dialled the number with shaky hands. She answered first time; I hadn't spoken to her for over 6 months. "Carol" she said "I knew you would find out". I started to shake, "so it's true" I wailed down the phone, the tears stung my eyes.

Ellie waddled in with her phooey shoe. I asked Carol to wait and got Ellie a book from her shelf. I sat her down and put C Beebies on. She didn't need to see me cry she had had enough of that. I went back to the phone "when did it happen"? "Why didn't anyone tell me"? "When's the funeral"? "I really want to go"?

The last time we spoke we argued I started to cry. "Grace you cant it's already happened he was buried yesterday with Peter his brother". I couldn't believe it; they had no intention of ever telling me, we didn't matter. I was so mad and upset I cried harder down the phone. Carol was silent. She went on to say; "I said to Mark Grace deserves to know" but he said "I can't be bothered with Grace right now". I was madder that she had even told me the last part, not the fact that he had said it. She should have kept that from me.

She said she had to go. I didn't know what to say. I told her to look after herself before putting the phone down. My hands were shaking, I desperately wanted to see him, to hug him, to be apart of the grief but it was too late, we had nothing to do with him or any of them anymore. I sat on the couch. I couldn't take it all in, he had had a massive heart attack, it was very quick and it wasn't expected. He had suffered with heart disease and he didn't know. I think as well as the attack along with it was a broken heart too. I felt immense grief and I had nobody to share it with, I didn't even get to say goodbye.

I rang Maria at work, she was about to tell me she couldn't talk when she heard me sob down the line. "Grace what's wrong" "it's Dave he's died" "Oh darling I am so sorry how old was he"? "He was in his seventies wasn't he"? Maria immediately thought it was Granddad like I did. "No Maria' Marks dad Dave".

The line went quiet for a moment, and then Maria burst in to tears too. When we were growing up she was always at his house and having a laugh with his dad and we went out and spent New Year together one year she knew the family like I did. We both cried together down the line. She was so shocked and promised she would be round to see me. I didn't go to work, and Ellie didn't go to school. I sat in a daze for the day.

As promised Kerrie rang me back, I cried to her, she was so shocked they hadn't even told me. "I wouldn't have gone if he didn't want me too",

"I would have gone afterwards, or it would have been nice just to know that he had gone", but to keep my distance. They were grieving. I was angry but I had to do something. I walked to the shop and bought Cards and ordered some flowers, I had no idea what to put, so I just put thinking of all of you, he was a lovely man and he was loved dearly thinking of you Grace and Ellie xx.

I sent the flowers the next day. There was no reply, I didn't expect one. I dropped Ellie off at school the next day; I got a taxi to the cemetery and bought a beautiful bouquet to take with me. I arrived and saw Dave's grave immediately, it had freshly covered soil over the top and there were mounds of flowers. There was one huge one with the words 'DAVE' and a small one that read Granddad. I forgot about His other baby; I looked at it and thought he was my little girl's granddad too. I put my flowers next to the ones that read granddad. I saw Emma's flowers and the huge card she had wrote to her dad. I read it and before id finished I was crying. She would be a complete mess I desperately wanted to see her, to hug her.

I sat down and told him that I hated that the last time we spoke it was strained and we had rowed. I said how sorry I was and walked away. I thought about the laughs we had had, him moaning about me cleaning the dust off his computer and how he would laugh at me when I balanced my tea on my pregnant belly. When I closed my eyes all I could see was his smile, and a song coming on the radio him beer in hand saying ' class', classic song' singing along to motown and UB40. I wished I could go back and tell him how much I loved him and I always thought of him like a second dad. But I couldn't he was gone.

I sat down and took a deep breath and had a long look at my life, and how much it had changed. Not so long ago I was sitting by the tree in my in laws with my huge pregnant bump, Mark's arms around me and Dave thinking of baby names. It was all so different the whole family had been torn apart, and the one thing that could never be changed was the fact that he was no longer here. Everything seems the same, but all the time it's changing even if we don't really see that it is.

My life I thought was one way, and now it's completely different. I never took a day for granted after that. I had wasted so much time concentrating on the past and loving someone who didn't give a toss about me or Ellie, the fact that he hadn't bothered to involve us in anything proved this, and I had what Carol had said ringing in my ears. "I can't be bothered with Grace right now". I felt like I had been hit with a truck every time I thought about it.

I deserved more than that. After all the years of being part of the family and having his child, I should have been told. He would only have had to say please stay away from the funeral and I would have. I decided that was it, I had enough of the guilt and the heartache. My life was just about to begin all over again. This thought excited me. It was the first time in along time I had been excited about anything. I felt like I had closed the chapter on Mark, I couldn't make him want to be a dad but I was damn well sure going to be a great Mum. I would love her enough for two people, and there are loads of single parent families that are fine. We have made it this far and we are happy. I looked at all the positives life could be hell of a lot worse. A lot of single mums are living in bed sits and temporary accommodation. I had a mortgage, my own house, it was nice and clean and it was mine it was ours. I had done it on my own and I never stopped to think about what I had achieved on my own. If anything it would teach my little girl, that if you work hard enough, you don't have to depend on other people to have what you want, if you want it you can go out and get it yourself.

Didn't realise until Maria had pointed that out to me I was teaching her from an early age to be strong and independent. I felt proud. I had always wanted to work with kids, even from a young age. I was bored with my job, I wanted more I had been there 4 years, did I want to be someone's skivvy for another 4? I was worth more than this. I decided to look for other things. I did some voluntary work at Ellie's school to get some experience, and did some youth work with the handicapped when I had spare time, I loved it. One morning I got up and decided I wanted to go see Dave at the grave, I had been thinking a lot about him. It wasn't really the day for it. It was freezing and windy and wet, but I wanted to go. I got the bus and walked up to the gates. I got some lovely roses and put them down. There were balloons and a little wind catcher, it looked pretty and kept nice. I told Dave I was going to begin again and get a life and look to the future not to the past, I told him I missed him and told him all about El, and I left a picture and a drawing of her by the flowers. There was a lady chattering away to a loved one in the grave beside me. She looked up and smiled and heard me talking, I felt a little embarrassed and a bit silly. She said: "they can hear us ya know". I just smiled and walked away.

The next morning I was late for work at least an hour late! Which meant Ellie was late! I raced down the stairs and got ready in record time. I hurried in to the offices and headed for my department. Hoping and praying my boss wasn't in the office, when I smacked bang in to a lad. I noticed him before I hit him with my arm.

'Sorry mate' I said and he turned round it was Glyn. A lad I had gone right the way through high school with, he was in my year and my class. He looked so different, not the way I remembered him. I remember his thick glasses and his blonde quiff hair, and he was as skinny as a bean pole. He was a lovely lad and I liked him in school, but he was a bit of a nerd I thought. He didn't look like that at all now, He was tall, chiselled looking with no hair, "shaved to the nut" as my dad would say. He had a lovely smile and big blue eyes and he wasn't a skinny whip anymore he looked really nice.

He remembered my name and said I looked exactly the same. What a compliment I thought as the last time I saw him I must have been eighteen, I looked very different now. Older, fatter, and probably wrinkled. He asked how I was and I asked how he was, he had been in before to sort out some benefits for he had just bought a house, and within weeks was laid off. He came back as he thought he had lost his watch. I said I would keep an eye out for it and if I found it I would give him a bell. He left his number on the counter. I smiled and said I had to get to work. "Have a happy Christmas Grace" he said and I did the oddest thing, something I did not do, I reached over and gave him a hug!

It was so awkward and I did not know why I had done this!! My face went red and in my head I thought "what the bloody hell did I do that for". I said; "you too", and hurried into the office. The boss was out, thank god, I didn't need another telling off this week. I hung up my coat and headed for the tea pot it was tea time already, I was sick of making this bloody tea I thought to myself. The girls covered for me and I thanked them. One of the girls asked what was up with me, I said nothing and mentioned that I had just seen a lad I went to school with and he had altered a lot, he looked nice. The girls teased me and said; "how long you have been single Grace"? "erm let me think... Forever"! "Then its time" they said, "Time for what"? "Time for you to get out there again". Oh no I knew what they meant, saying he was nice was one thing, being set up with someone I hadn't seen for 10 years was another. If we find his watch let me know though and I will ring him.

I went to my desk and thought nothing more about it. Then there was a phone call. I never got phone calls I was the gofer. I took messages and had the occasional call from the school or Maria or my Mum pretending to be important messages, other than that no phone calls. Even with that I knew there was something fishy as all the girls eyes were staring at me and leaning over my desk Sam who sat in front of me was smiling.

"Phone call Grace" I took the phone and said "hello". 'Erm hi Grace its Glyn' "you know the one you spoke to before"? "'Oh yeah hi we haven't been able to find your watch I said". "I was ringing to see if you wanted to go out tonight"? I panicked and said "no" he sounded gutted, "I have got a little girl and ill need to arrange a babysitter" I said.

Within seconds all you could hear was "ill have Ellie grace" "ill have Ellie". I was desperately embarrassed, and wanted the ground to swallow me up. It was hard enough speaking to a man on the phone but with 20 pair of eyes staring at me it was even harder. I arranged to meet him the next day. I put down the phone they all gasped and came over and squeezed me smiling. "Who the bloody hell set that up", they all blamed each other and then the boss walked in everyone was back to looking like they were doing something.

I felt sick the next day, we were meeting in a local pub and I decided I wasn't going. My friend Laura was having Ellie and she practically pushed me out of the door. "Have fun" she said and don't come back early. I was 27 years old and I felt like I was going on a first date when I was 16. I had only ever had one serious boyfriend and I couldn't imagine being with anyone else. I rang Maria on my mobile for support. "Grace what's the worst that can happen"? "He could turn out to be an axe murderer"? "Or worst still find me boring".

She was great she told me how lovely I was, and he would be lucky to have a date with me. By the time I got off the phone to her she had me thinking I was a bloody super model. I loved that girl, she always knew what to say to me and she always somehow made everything better. I made my way to the local pub; I thought what the hell am I doing here?? I wanted to turn and walk away and then Maria rang. "Don't even think about it" "just go inside and if it doesn't work out you could gain a new friend". She knew me so well. Okay I took a deep breath and went inside.

The place was buzzing for a Thursday night and people were coming and going. The bar was busy and I looked around. I couldn't see him. "Oh my god" "I have been stood up" "he didn't even turn up". My face was red I turned round ready to walk out when I saw him sitting in the comfy chairs in the corner of the pub, he stood up and waved, on the table next to him there were two drinks one for him and one for me. I walked over red faced and I didn't know how to greet him, he didn't know how to greet me it was awkward so I just patted his arm and said hello. He smiled and said' "I didn't know what you drank so I just ordered you a wine is that okay"? "Err yes I love wine". It was true I did love wine but it didn't love me, I was a lightweight. The type of person that could go out on a tenner come back drunk as a skunk and still has change.

I sat down and he had already finished his drink, he looked as nervous as I did and he went to get another. He came back with another glass of wine for me; I hadn't even touched the first. He came back and said how nice I looked and we talked about school and what he had been up too. It was nice but we were both really nervous I began drinking my wine for Dutch courage, as we talked and we started to feel more comfortable with one another the wine flowed.

I felt myself beginning to get dizzy, I had Ellie to look after when I got in and I had to get up for work the next day. He bought me another. I sipped it this time. He talked about the army, what jobs he did when he left school, and I talked about Ellie and what id been up too. He made me laugh, and he was very gentle.

He showed me pictures on his phone of where he had worked and silly photo's of him with his mates. I realised we were sitting very close to each other on the big comfy couch our arms touching. We seemed to both realise this at the same time. At the beginning of the night there was a huge space between us and now we were talking like we had kept in touch for years. I felt relaxed but very drunk. I hadn't been drunk in ages. It felt strange. Glyn was mortified. "I wasn't trying t get you drunk honestly I am sorry you have had too much wine".

I staggered to my feet. He hailed a cab and we got in I "I need to go home" I said. "Ill take you there and then ill go home". "Okay" I said. "One problem" "what"? "I don't know where you live"? "Oh" I told him and off we went.

He had hold of my bag and said that would it be okay to have my number and he would ring to see if I was okay tomorrow. I said "yes" and he helped me out of the taxi and dropped me at the house. He apologised to my babysitter and explained I had had too much to drink. He got back in the cab and went home himself. Laura laughed when she saw me and helped me get undressed. She made sure I was okay before I locked the door. Within half an hour I had a text off him saying "I enjoyed tonight your easy to talk too and I would love to meet up again Glyn" x'

I was thrilled. I checked on Ellie, Laura said she had been fine and not woken up once. Her quilt was not on her, and her skin felt cold, I covered her up and kissed her goodnight. A cup of coffee is what I need that will sort me out I thought. I went to the kitchen but before I got there I threw up all over my new rug. I couldn't believe it. I didn't have the strength or stomach to clean it and binned it. I instantly felt better for throwing up but had a banging headache. I went to bed and text Glyn back. I said that I enjoyed the night too, and would love to meet again I told him I hadn't been on a date in a very long time and that id been very hurt. He text back don't worry it will just be nice to be with you. I thought that was lovely, and with my banging head I drifted off to sleep wondering if Dave would approve.

Chapter 24

MOVING ON

We saw each other lots and we had been on 4 dates now. What I loved more than anything was the fact that he never tried to kiss me or push himself on me. He was lovely. There was one thing that bothered me though, at times I thought he was ignoring me then one day when we were walking through the town centre he said: ' do you mind walking on the other side of me I am deaf in this ear'. I started to laugh; he looked at me like I had two heads. 'What are you laughing at'? I told him how I thought he was ignoring me or thought I was boring or both. Then he started to laugh to.

I didn't feel any pressure being with him he was so laid back he was practically horizontal. Then one day we went to his new house he was watching TV in his room as he had not had his couch delivered yet. 'What you watching?' he told me he was watching 'Good Will Hunting' I loved that film can I come watch it with you? He looked horrified, ill lie on top of the bed you can get in if you want?

The room was freezing and he was just being nice. 'Oh I didn't mean like that I just meant to keep warm' he was tripping over his words he looked so cute and I had this urge to hug him. But I didn't. I smiled and said its okay I knew what you meant. I had talked about Ellie loads to him and showed him a picture of her. He said she was beautiful. I didn't want them to be introduced till I knew what was going on with 'us' if there were was ever going to be a 'us' I had plenty of time I was just enjoying his company. I was so cold I ended up zipping my coat up and wrapping his duvet around me. 'Sorry the heating will come on soon it's so cold up here' I nodded and we watched the film. Then we started talking and in the end we were facing each other chatting about everything and anything. Then he said when I get my couch we can snuggle up and get popcorn and watch a film if you like. Then I said something that shocked me." I have to wait till you get your couch for you to snuggle me"

His face went bright red, I kept smiling this was me flirting! I was crap at this, and crap at boys, but I was doing it I was making him embarrassed not the other way round. He sat next to me and then got closer with his arm around me. He then said' how's that?' "Nice" got even closer and said how's that He smiled and then I said" doo I have to wait till you get your couch for you to kiss me" He laughed and then I kissed him!

This wasn't me I didn't do this and the last time I had kissed anyone it was Mark. It was nice his mouth felt different and his face wasn't familiar but it was nice I missed being touched and kissed. Then I suddenly stopped. I thought about El, and I felt guilty what was I doing? I talked to him about a lot of things and he listened. We ended up kissing again, and pretty soon the bedroom was hot. "not taking my jeans off' I said. He smiled and said "okay you don't have too do anything you don't want to do" he said. Within two hours I was in my underwear and so was he, and we were locked in each others arms. He commented on my body and my skin and said how lovely it was. I hid my jelly belly from his view and he moved my hands away. "Am covered in stretch marks "said my tummy looks like the map of china. He laughed and kissed my belly I laughed to myself just like Shirley Valentine I thought. I wanted to touch him and make love I hadn't in such a long time. He was very excited and said are you sure? I said yes and I asked him to use something he said yes of course and he quickly got up and was looking through boxes and he hit his head on the door, trying to cover his body as he rubbed it. He was so clumsy even more so than me. We were like a pair well matched.

He was and still is one of the gentlest people I have ever met. I peeked at him putting it on and looked at his body it was different to Mark's his back, his legs it all looked so different. I didn't want to compare but I had only ever really had one serious boyfriend before this was all alien and strange to me, but in a good way. He kissed every part of my body and was so gentle and loving. It was nice and we lay next to each other and he tickled my arms. 'So much for me not taking my jeans off and taking it slow' I said out loud. If this is what you do on a fourth date, what the hell do you do on a 5th date! He said laughing and I hit him with the pillow.

I reassured him I wasn't like that and this was all very new and different to me, that I didn't do things like this. He smiled and said that he was teasing me.

He told me of his hurt and a girl he nearly married. I understood his pain immediately and I saw the familiar look of agony in his eyes when he talked about it. We swapped painful memories and we both ended up making each other laugh. We had so much in common and yet we were so different. We had both been hurt and were both lonely. Just before Christmas I told him I wanted to meet Ellie and he was very interested and excited about seeing her.

He bought her a teddy that smelled of chocolate and put it in a huge shiny purple bag; he remembered that this was her favourite colour. I thought it was such a sweet thing to do. I got him a teddy and a card and some chocolate and I decided we were going to go to Pizza Hut and I would introduce her to my new friend. I felt nervous about them meeting but Ellie was my world and always with me, and whenever I wanted to see Glyn she couldn't be with me because they hadn't met yet. I didn't like anything being separate from her; the timing had to be right.

He asked if he could come to the house and drop off her gift Christmas Eve night. He knew she would be in bed so he said ill come about ten and have a cuppa then leave. I agreed and thought he could take his gift too to have it there for Christmas morning. We chatted on the couch, and then I heard Ellie shouting my name coming down the stairs. 'Oh god' was my first reaction she comes down the stairs and sees mummy with a strange man, will she look back on it and think mummy was a slapper? As she made her way down the stairs lots of different things went through my head. But the biggest one was guilt. It wasn't her Dad, it was someone else. He had moved on big time and Ellie didn't even remember him. What if it didn't work out with Glyn? The panic in my voice grew worse. Glyn picked up on it straight away. 'Don't worry ill go in the kitchen' he said and she toddled in yawning. 'What are you doing up madam I said' kissing her cheek. She was nearly 5, the following February.

Time had gone so quick my baby was getting so big. 'I need a drink mummy' I need you to cuddle me' 'okay baby' I said and picked her up and placed her on my hip. Her legs wrapped around my body. She was getting heavy I will have to stop doing this or I would have no back left I thought to myself. She saw the purple bag and ran to it I forgot it was there. No Ellie wait. It was too late She turned around and saw Glyn. 'Ellie this is my friend Glyn' 'hiya' she said can I have a drink now mum'?

Was her reply. Glyn said that he was glad to meet her and showed her the teddy in the bag. 'This is for you' he said and handed it to her. She sniffed it and snuggled it straight away. 'Thank you' she said 'can I take it to bed Mummy'. Okay I said and smiled. She clung to my leg I took her back to bed and within minutes she was asleep again. Glyn said she was gorgeous and looked just like me.

We were very happy and not long after Ellie's birthday he became a permanent fixture. He is a massive part of my life and Ellie's... I love him to bits and Ellie does too.

He thinks of himself as Ellie's step Dad. Which is a responsibility he has taken seriously, and I think is lovely of him. He says he loves her unconditionally and always will. Just like a real dad should. She adores him and him her. Whatever happens we will always be a family he says, Glyn's the nicest person you could ever meet. I never thought I would be in a relationship again, I really didn't, I didn't go looking for it, and I ended up meeting and being with a lovely man. It hasn't always been plain sailing between us, and in the beginning I didn't treat him as well as I should have. I was so hurt and so full of anger I directed it all towards him. But he stayed because he loves me. I am very lucky in lots of ways.

There comes a time when you have to let go of the past and start again and make new memories. I was so fixated on what I had lost that I didn't stop to think about what I had already. I have a beautiful daughter who will and has always come first. I feel like I have grown as a person. I realised you have to love yourself first before your lucky enough for someone else to love you back. I don't think things are set in stone anymore, and I don't think life will be rosy. I wanted to get married so young and have a house with the white picket fence. I can honestly say that I don't want that. What I have got is a lot of friends and family that love me, a gorgeous little girl, a house but no picket fence. I don't want the fairy tale. All I want is a chance to live and be happy. Be happy for me not for someone else. I am happy with the lot that I have and all my experiences have made me who I am today and better for it. We moved again I sold my house the one in the not so great area, and I got Ellie in to a fantastic school. We live in a cull de sac in a nice area and not far From Ellie's school. I moved jobs and took a risk. I went back to college and now work within a Learning Support Department within a High School helping to educate Children with Special Needs. I have been there 3 years. I passed all my courses and am able to stand on my own two feet. I am happy and contented with my lot.

There are women all over the world that think they will never cope by themselves; I never thought I ever could, but guess what you can. If I can do it with all the stress I had to cope with then anyone can. I feel like I can deal with anything and get through it. I feel very lucky to have had support around me and love, as it is what helped me to get better. There is still a stigma or a label with Mental Illness. It can happen to anyone anywhere at any time in their lives and I don't just mean the Post Natal Kind. If someone breaks their leg, you expect a cast to be put on and it heal and the person gets better. It is exactly the same with Mental Illness if you seek help and get the right medication, a person can heal and they can get better. I used to feel embarrassed by my illness, but now am proud that I lived through it.

I think that it is disgusting in today's society that there is a conveyer belt system of care in Hospitals. People have babies and within 6 hours some mothers are sent home. How can this happen? It's like 'your done' 'next'. There have been so many mothers who have been sent home because they haven't been closely monitored for signs of PND. There have been mothers who haven't even realised it themselves, and have taken their own lives and the lives of their children. These stories are rare but do happen and are tragic. They are a statistic of the system that's failing them. More should be done. The government should recognise that PND is becoming more common in this country, and hospitals need more training and awareness of this condition, and what this condition can lead too if not looked at and treated properly. Yes lots of people have babies and the majority are fine, go home and they have their experience of motherhood. But there are so many women who don't.

Since having my PND experience, I have spoken to lots of women, all different ages, backgrounds, etc that have suffered with this terrible illness that can affect anyone who has a baby. My experience of becoming a mother was awful, and that is something that I hate to say and admit, as I love and adore my little girl. I have said before, I felt robbed of something that was rightfully mine, and will never get that back. When pregnant, and in Labour the staff that looked after me were fantastic. I felt so looked after, and I felt my baby did too once she came. However the staff that looked after me once she was born and taken on to the ward was a different story. Looking back, I had the signs of PND and that something was wrong, I told a nurse she looked like an angel! And was still allowed home. I was ill, physically and mentally, and yet "I had to pull myself together and look after my baby" It angers me when I think back; I was struggling, physically and emotionally. But told to go home as they needed the bed. Even after the traumatic birth,

Rash etc.

I ideally would like things to be changed where hospitals are concerned when people have babies. The care that is there for mothers and babies on the labour ward should still be there and be as just as important when women have had their babies. From my experience I would like to give a message to sufferers not to suffer in silence, to tell someone as soon as they can how they feel, and get help. This is vital and so important to the bond they have with their babies, and for their own sanity. You are not alone, there are other people who feel like you, and if help is sought you will get better. Advice to families, partners, mothers, in-laws etc. Remember to listen to your loved one who is going through something like this. They may not be the person they have always been whilst going through this illness, but they are still there and will come back. They need support, love and don't need someone taking over, and making decisions for them. It is nice to be consulted about decisions and feel in the loop, even though they might not be able to cope, it's important your loved ones have a feeling of control. Doing everything for the baby that's been born, to save the mother 'the trouble' 'to help' will not help; it will make a situation much worse. I can't speak for everyone as people can have a certain type, and everybody is different. However this condition is so over powering, de humanising almost, the help that women get, and the type that they get not just from the doctors from everyone involved with them is so important.

Because I was sectioned, and so ill, I had to be monitored by staff, which would look through my glass, glare at me, check on me and wait until the next member of staff would come to take over. This was their job. However one day a nurse knocked on my door, popped her head round and said she was sorry but she would be monitoring me for the next half an hour, she knew it was intrusive but she wanted to let me know she was there. Just this single act alone, made me feel like a person again. As much as it was their job to make sure I was safe and my baby was safe, I was being told first hand, it was like I was still a person and it wasn't their god given right. It was the only time and the first time a member of staff had ever done that. It made me feel like I had a say, I was important, and I think it is important, to not let go of the respect for someone who has lost themselves even in a unit. It can make all the difference to someone.

Friends and Families should be there to lean on each other for support as well as being there for the person that's sick, as it can be so upsetting seeing your loved one go through it, so make sure you get support and help yourselves. Get advice, speak to staff and doctors, even go on the net and look at it in detail if it gives you more of an understanding. To remember that they will get better eventually.

Keeping a routine when your loved one comes home I would say is a good idea, as that's what they have been used to in the hospital setting. Keep things calm. Don't have all the family and friends round all at once. Keep visits in the hospital and even when you come home to a minimum of people, and don't let them stay so long, it can be very tiring for the person that they have come to see.

I wrote this book for me, for my daughter, and for my family who saw me go through the worst experience of my life. I also wrote it for other women who may have or may in the future experience this terrible illness. I also decided to share what happened along the way, as that is just as important as the medical condition. People leave people, people have affairs, people hurt, and go it alone. Generally people get on with it, and don't want to talk about it, I decided to share what I went through, and how I felt. It is a "warts and all" look at what happened to me and how I got better and how I got through it. If it helps one person to think 'she did it, I can do it' that's exactly the reason I put as much in my book as I did. I am a better person, a better mummy and I would say a lot more accepting of change having gone through this.

In writing this I hope to change people's attitudes to mental illness, and instil that it can happen to the sanest of people. I hope people, will realise that having a baby is not a walk in the park for everyone. I would love to change the amount of time that new mums have in hospital following giving birth, but this is not a feat I think I can do by myself! If my book raises eyebrows, and prompts questions and makes people become more aware, it will have been worth it.

Right now I look forward to my future, I don't know what it will hold, but I am excited to find out, I am no longer a 'victim' I am and always will be a survivor of this terrible illness, and I know that I am not hopeless or useless or alone. I got through that and if I did I can get through anything, I survived and I am here.

Grace Sharrock

THIS LITTLE PERSON...

This little person that depends on me...
From a babe she's grown, as lovely as can be.

I never thought I could ever have this bond,
The love that I feel has grown so strong.

Her little hand that slips into mine,
I'm so glad Am her mummy, even though it took time.

Her Blue eyes that sparkle
When she laughs, when she sings,
She is a piece of my heart and means everything.

I am so glad that she's here,
This little person, who I hold so very dear.

Through all the heartache, agony, trouble and strife,
She's my heart, she's my darling, and she's my whole life.

Grace Sharrock

Printed in Great Britain
by Amazon.co.uk, Ltd.,
Marston Gate.